FRANK STEWART'S

Bridge Club

Foreword by Eddie Kantar

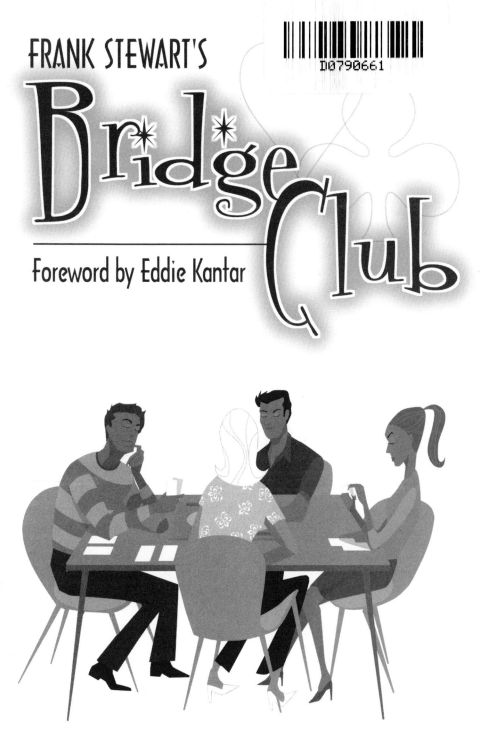

MASTER POINT PRESS ▸ TORONTO

D0790661

Master Point Press
331 Douglas Ave.
Toronto, Ontario Canada
M5M 1H2
(416) 781-0351 Fax (416) 781-1831
Internet www.masterpointpress.com

Canadian Cataloguing in Publication Data
Frank Stewart 1946-
Frank Stewart's Bridge Club/Frank Stewart
ISBN 1-894154-58-4

1. Contract bridge − Defensive play. 1 Title.
GV1282.3 2.S835 2003   795.41'5   C2003-902596-9

Editor	Ray Lee
Cover and interior design	Olena S. Sullivan/New Mediatrix
Interior format and copyediting	Deanna Bourassa

Printed and bound in Canada by Webcom Canada Ltd.

1 2 3 4 5 6 7   07 06 05 04 03

Contents

You've made your first good move by buying this book. Let me tell you why. First and foremost are the hands, I call them "theme" hands; they are practical because they come up frequently. These hands, clearly explained, are perfect for the intermediate or advanced intermediate player wanting to move up a notch. (Lives there an intermediate player who doesn't think of him or herself as an advanced intermediate player?) The hands are so good that I have committed the ultimate flattery, I have "lifted" several to use as examples in my classes.

As if this weren't enough, the introductions to each column do credit to a stand-up comedian. Where Frank gets these opening salvos, I have no idea, but they are funny. This is not to mention the characters roaming around the pages. These are types we can remember from our own experiences. (I even recognized myself now and then!)

I was also impressed with the format. First you are presented with a number of two-handed problems, usually play problems, with the North-South hands shown. This eliminates the need to cover up the unseen hands where at times you can't help but see a card or three. After you answer the problem (correctly of course), you can turn to a later page to check to see whether Frank was clever enough to come up with the same solution. If perchance there should happen to be a discrepancy, believe Frank.

If this book was meant to be both instructive and entertaining, as Frank hoped, put me down for an A+.

Eddie Kantar

FRANK STEWART'S
Bridge Club

To Jim Lanson,

All the best to you

Frank Stewart

PART 1

Winter

1. January 4   Tangled Webb

East dealer
N-S vulnerable

$\spadesuit$ 8 5
$\heartsuit$ A J 10 9 8
$\diamond$ A K Q
$\clubsuit$ A J 10

$\spadesuit$ A 9 6 3
$\heartsuit$ 6
$\diamond$ J 9 2
$\clubsuit$ K 9 8 6 3

West	North	East	South
		1$\spadesuit$	pass
pass	dbl	pass	2$\clubsuit$
pass	2$\heartsuit$	pass	2NT
pass	3NT	all pass	

West leads the ten of spades. Plan the play.

2. January 8   Regular Partnerships

South dealer
N-S vulnerable

$\spadesuit$ —
$\heartsuit$ K J 9 7 6 4
$\diamond$ A K 3 2
$\clubsuit$ 6 5 3

$\spadesuit$ K 5 3
$\heartsuit$ A Q 10 8 2
$\diamond$ 5 4
$\clubsuit$ A Q 7

West	North	East	South
			1$\heartsuit$
2$\spadesuit$	3$\spadesuit$	4$\spadesuit$	pass
pass	6$\heartsuit$	all pass	

West leads the queen of spades. Plan the play.

3. January 10

South dealer
Both vulnerable

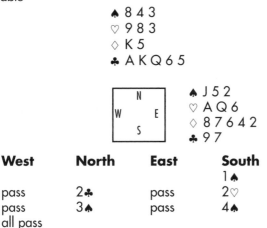

```
            ♠ 8 4 3
            ♡ 9 8 3
            ◇ K 5
            ♣ A K Q 6 5

                           ♠ J 5 2
          N                ♡ A Q 6
        W   E              ◇ 8 7 6 4 2
          S                ♣ 9 7
```

West	North	East	South
			1♠
pass	2♣	pass	2♡
pass	3♠	pass	4♠
all pass			

West leads the queen of diamonds. South takes the ace, cashes the jack of clubs, leads a club to the ace and continues with the queen. How do you defend?

4. January 13

South dealer
E-W vulnerable

```
            ♠ Q 10 8 6 5
            ♡ 8 6 4 3
            ◇ Q 9 5 2
            ♣ —


            ♠ J 9 7 4 2
            ♡ A Q J
            ◇ 7 4
            ♣ A K 10
```

West	North	East	South
			1♠
pass	4♠	all pass	

West leads the queen of clubs. Plan the play.

1. January 4

East dealer
N-S vulnerable

```
                    ♠ 8 5
                    ♡ A J 10 9 8
                    ◇ A K Q
                    ♣ A J 10
        ♠ 10 4                      ♠ K Q J 7 2
        ♡ 7 4 3 2         N         ♡ K Q 5
        ◇ 10 8 6 5 3   W     E      ◇ 7 4
        ♣ 5 4             S         ♣ Q 7 2
                    ♠ A 9 6 3
                    ♡ 6
                    ◇ J 9 2
                    ♣ K 9 8 6 3
```

West	North	East	South
		1♠	pass
pass	dbl	pass	2♣
pass	2♡	pass	2NT
pass	3NT	all pass	

Opening lead: ♠10

My bridge club has 600 members. We comprise plenty of nondescript Browns and Smiths, but, as you'd suppose, there are also a Mr. North and a Mrs. West — who always occupy their namesake seats. We have a Diamond, a Hart, a Deal and a Card, and there are fitting partnerships: Singleton-King and Long-Short. Dr. Bidwell is known for remorseless accuracy in the auction, and curmudgeonly old Mrs. Passmore is legendary for the soundness of her overcalls.

Then there is Tom Webb, known as 'Tangle', who seems to run into blocked suits more often than anyone else. As South, Tom won the second spade and started the clubs, intending to finesse through East as an avoidance play. But when he took the ace and led the jack, East alertly covered with the queen.

'Tangle' was entangled like a box of coat hangers. If he ducked to keep a link with his hand, East would run the spades. If instead South took the king and ten of clubs, he couldn't get back for the other clubs. He'd have only eight tricks, and East would get in with the king of hearts to run the spades.

If you were South, could you get untangled and make 3NT?

South must win the third spade, pitching dummy's queen of diamonds. He takes the A-K of diamonds and the ace of clubs and leads the jack of clubs. East must cover to cause a problem, and South takes the king. South can then discard the blocking ten of clubs on the jack of diamonds and run the clubs.

2. January 8 — Regular Partnerships

South dealer
N-S vulnerable

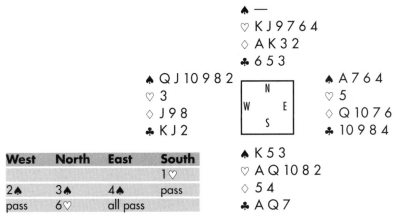

```
                        ♠ —
                        ♡ K J 9 7 6 4
                        ◇ A K 3 2
                        ♣ 6 5 3
   ♠ Q J 10 9 8 2                        ♠ A 7 6 4
   ♡ 3              ┌─────────┐          ♡ 5
   ◇ J 9 8         W│    N    │E         ◇ Q 10 7 6
   ♣ K J 2          │    S    │          ♣ 10 9 8 4
                    └─────────┘
                        ♠ K 5 3
                        ♡ A Q 10 8 2
                        ◇ 5 4
                        ♣ A Q 7
```

West	North	East	South
			1♡
2♠	3♠	4♠	pass
pass	6♡	all pass	

Opening lead: ♠Q

My club, like any other, has many regular partnerships: for instance, a doctor-pharmacist pair who do well (except when the pharmacist can't read the doc's signals). In this deal, North-South were a dentist and a manicurist we call 'Tooth and Nail' because that's how they argue.

Tooth, South, ruffed the first spade in dummy, drew trumps and tried a club finesse with the queen. West took the king and got another club later to beat the slam. The argument began immediately.

Tooth: 'What kind of bid was six hearts? What if I'd had two low clubs?'

Nail: 'When you didn't double four spades, I thought you had little strength in spades and therefore something in clubs.'

Tooth: 'Bid five diamonds over four spades. Let me decide.'

Nail: 'I wanted to be in six hearts. Why dally?'

Nobody realized declarer could Nail down the slam by throwing one club from dummy at Trick 1 and another on the king of spades later. And that's the whole Tooth and nothing but.

Bidding Quiz

YOU HOLD: ♠ A 7 6 4 ♡ 5 ◇ Q 10 7 6 ♣ 10 9 8 4. Your partner opens one heart, you respond one spade and he then bids two diamonds. The opponents pass. What do you say?

ANSWER: Pass. Since partner did not jump to three diamonds, he has fewer than 18 points, and game is almost impossible. If you raise to three diamonds, partner will expect about 11 points from you and will go on to game (and go down) if he has 15 or more points.

Bald Statements

South dealer
Both vulnerable

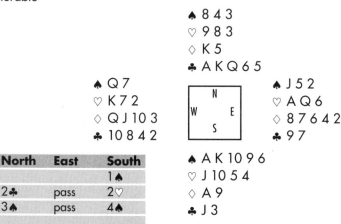

♠ 8 4 3
♡ 9 8 3
◇ K 5
♣ A K Q 6 5

♠ Q 7
♡ K 7 2
◇ Q J 10 3
♣ 10 8 4 2

N
W E
S

♠ J 5 2
♡ A Q 6
◇ 8 7 6 4 2
♣ 9 7

♠ A K 10 9 6
♡ J 10 5 4
◇ A 9
♣ J 3

West	North	East	South
			1♠
pass	2♣	pass	2♡
pass	3♠	pass	4♠
all pass			

Opening lead: ◇Q

The club member we call 'Grapefruit' got his nickname not only for his eternally sour disposition but because his head is as bald as a mountaintop in January. 'Some men wear their hair parted,' is how Cy the Cynic puts it. 'Grapefruit's is de-parted.'

Grapefruit, West, led the queen of diamonds against South's game. South won with the ace and could have cashed the A-K of trumps and started the clubs, hoping to discard two hearts before the defender with the missing high trump ruffed. But South had a different idea: he started the clubs at Trick 2.

On the third club, East ruffed with the deuce of trumps — and the defenders' chances departed. South overruffed, drew trumps, got to dummy with the king of diamonds and threw hearts on the last two clubs for an overtrick. The bald facts, as Grapefruit pointed out in his usual acid tone, were that East must ruff the third club with the jack of trumps. South overruffs but still loses three hearts and a trump.

Bidding Quiz

YOU HOLD: ♠ 8 4 3 ♡ 9 8 3 ◇ K 5 ♣ A K Q 6 5. Your partner opens one diamond, you respond two clubs and he rebids two diamonds. The opponents pass. What do you say?

ANSWER: Raise to three diamonds, inviting game. Though partner may have been obliged to rebid a five-card suit, you have no choice: a rebid of three clubs would promise longer clubs and wouldn't encourage him to bid game; a bid of 2NT would suggest strength in the unbid suits.

4. January 13

South dealer
E-W vulnerable

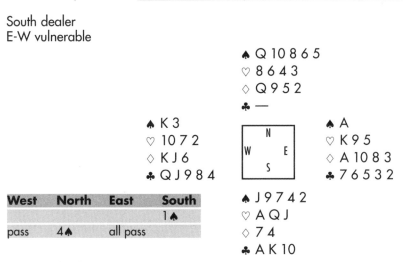

♠ Q 10 8 6 5
♡ 8 6 4 3
◇ Q 9 5 2
♣ —

♠ K 3
♡ 10 7 2
◇ K J 6
♣ Q J 9 8 4

♠ A
♡ K 9 5
◇ A 10 8 3
♣ 7 6 5 3 2

♠ J 9 7 4 2
♡ A Q J
◇ 7 4
♣ A K 10

West	North	East	South
			1♠
pass	4♠	all pass	

Opening lead: ♣Q

When a new member of my club asked me how Cy the Cynic got his nickname, I wrote down today's deal, which I'd watched the day before.

Cy was South at one table of a team match. His game contract looked hopeless, but Cy ruffed the first club in dummy, led a heart to his queen, ruffed his king of clubs, won another heart finesse with the jack and cashed the ace. When hearts broke 3-3, Cy got back to dummy by ruffing the ace of clubs and led the thirteenth heart.

If East ruffed with the ace, Cy would throw a diamond, losing two trumps and a diamond. When East discarded, Cy threw a diamond. West ruffed, but Cy later crashed the defenders' high trumps.

'Well played,' our new member remarked. 'Surely his team gained points on that deal.'
'At the second table,' I told him, 'South won the first club with the king and led a trump. West for Cy's team put up the king, and South lost a trump and two diamonds: a push.'

'I begin to understand,' said our newcomer.

Bidding Quiz

YOU HOLD: ♠ A ♡ K 9 5 ◇ A 10 8 3 ♣ 7 6 5 3 2. Your partner opens one spade, you bid two clubs, he rebids two spades and you try 2NT. Partner next bids three hearts. What do you say?

ANSWER: Bid three spades or, with a timid partner, four spades. Partner has a minimum opening bid with six spades and four hearts. (If he had extra strength or only five spades, his second bid would have been two hearts.) Play in the 6-1 fit.

5. January 20   Wendy the Feminist

East dealer
E-W vulnerable

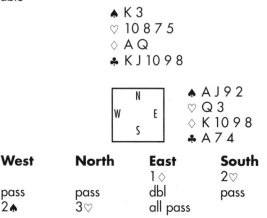

        ♠ K 3
        ♡ 10 8 7 5
        ◇ A Q
        ♣ K J 10 9 8

                        ♠ A J 9 2
                        ♡ Q 3
                        ◇ K 10 9 8
                        ♣ A 7 4

West	North	East	South
		1◇	2♡
pass	pass	dbl	pass
2♠	3♡	all pass	

West leads the seven of spades, and dummy plays the three. How do you defend?

6. January 22   Major Disaster

South dealer
N-S vulnerable

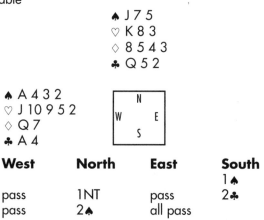

        ♠ J 7 5
        ♡ K 8 3
        ◇ 8 5 4 3
        ♣ Q 5 2

♠ A 4 3 2
♡ J 10 9 5 2
◇ Q 7
♣ A 4

West	North	East	South
			1♠
pass	1NT	pass	2♣
pass	2♠	all pass	

You lead the jack of hearts, winning, and another heart. South discards a diamond and discards another diamond when East leads the ace of hearts next. East shifts to the deuce of diamonds, but South produces the ace and then leads the king of trumps. How do you defend?

7. January 26   The Killing Lead

South dealer
Neither vulnerable

```
          ♠ Q 10
          ♡ 4 3 2
          ◊ 10 9 7 6
          ♣ A K J 10

          ♠ A 4 2
          ♡ A 8 7 6 5
          ◊ A
          ♣ Q 8 7 6
```

West	North	East	South
			1♡
pass	2♣	pass	3♣
pass	3♡	pass	4♡
all pass			

West leads the ten of hearts, and East plays the jack. Plan the play.

8. January 29   Even Disposition

North dealer
Both vulnerable

```
          ♠ Q 9 6 4 3
          ♡ —
          ◊ A 7 6 5
          ♣ K 9 8 7

          ♠ A 10 8 7 5
          ♡ A 3
          ◊ K J 2
          ♣ A J 6
```

West	North	East	South
	pass	pass	1♠
2♡	3♡	pass	4♣
pass	4◊	pass	5♠
pass	6♠	all pass	

West leads the king of hearts. Plan the play.

5. January 20 — Wendy the Feminist

East dealer
E-W vulnerable

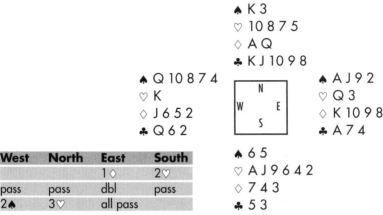

```
                          ♠ K 3
                          ♡ 10 8 7 5
                          ◇ A Q
                          ♣ K J 10 9 8
      ♠ Q 10 8 7 4                      ♠ A J 9 2
      ♡ K                               ♡ Q 3
      ◇ J 6 5 2           N             ◇ K 10 9 8
      ♣ Q 6 2         W       E         ♣ A 7 4
                          S
                          ♠ 6 5
                          ♡ A J 9 6 4 2
                          ◇ 7 4 3
                          ♣ 5 3
```

West	North	East	South
		1◇	2♡
pass	pass	dbl	pass
2♠	3♡	all pass	

Opening lead: ♠7

Fireworks were expected when Cy the Cynic, who thinks a woman's place is in the kitchen, opposed Wendy the Feminist, a new member of my club. (Ask Wendy how many men it takes to wallpaper a room, and she'll say three — if you slice them thinly.)

As South, Cy played low from dummy on the first spade, and Wendy, East, took the jack and ace and led a low trump. Cy took the ace and led a club to the jack. Wendy ducked (best), but Cy led the king(!) from dummy next and could set up the clubs, losing a club, two spades and a trump.

'Even a man should know enough to lead the suit his partner bid,' Wendy told West. 'A diamond lead beats it.'

'No,' said Cy. 'I still set up the clubs, and you get one trick in each suit. A spade lead works — if you play the deuce. You know from the Rule of Eleven that I can't beat the seven. If West wins the first spade, a diamond shift sinks me.'

First blood to Cy. 'Wendy can dish it out,' he told me, 'but she can't cook it.'

Bidding Quiz

YOU HOLD: ♠ K 3 ♡ 10 8 7 5 ◇ A Q ♣ K J 10 9 8. The dealer, on your right, opens one spade. You double, and your partner bids two diamonds. The opponents pass. What do you say?

ANSWER: Pass. A good partner would have had the decency to respond with a bid in hearts or clubs, but good partners are hard to find. Since you have no extra strength, you can't afford to act again although your diamond support isn't what it should be.

6. January 22   Major Disaster

South dealer
N-S vulnerable

```
                          ♠ J 7 5
                          ♡ K 8 3
                          ◇ 8 5 4 3
                          ♣ Q 5 2
        ♠ A 4 3 2                        ♠ 6
        ♡ J 10 9 5 2          N          ♡ A Q 7 6
        ◇ Q 7           W          E     ◇ K J 9 2
        ♣ A 4                S           ♣ 9 8 7 3
                          ♠ K Q 10 9 8
                          ♡ 4
                          ◇ A 10 6
                          ♣ K J 10 6
```

West	North	East	South
			1♠
pass	1NT	pass	2♣
pass	2♠	all pass	

Opening lead: ♡J

'It was the mother of all disasters,' a player at the club told me grimly. 'We sold out to two spades when we could make five hearts.'

'And then,' his partner added, 'they made two spades.'

South had refused to ruff the second heart; he threw a diamond, then another diamond when East led the ace of hearts.

East next led a diamond, and South won and led a high trump. West took the ace and led the queen of diamonds, and South ruffed and forced out the ace of clubs. West, with no more diamonds, led a heart, but South ruffed in dummy, drew trumps and claimed the contract.

'Which one of us should have bid?' East and West asked.

'Unclear,' was my verdict. 'West didn't have enough to try two hearts at his first turn but might have bid after North-South stopped low. East might have doubled 1NT for takeout.'

It is clear that West can save something by defeating two spades. If he holds up his ace of trumps until the third lead, he can force South to ruff a heart in his hand, losing control. He can also prevail by winning the second trump and leading the ◇Q.

Bidding Quiz

YOU HOLD: ♠ A 4 3 2 ♡ J 10 9 5 2 ◇ Q 7 ♣ A 4. Dealer, on your left, opens one spade. Your partner doubles, and the next player raises to two spades. What do you say?

ANSWER: Bid four hearts (or, with a fine partner, cuebid three spades to show the strength for game). Your partner promises a good hand with heart support and is sure to have a singleton spade when the opponents have bid and raised spades. You'll make game easily.

The Killing Lead

South dealer
Neither vulnerable

```
              ♠ Q 10
              ♡ 4 3 2
              ◇ 10 9 7 6
              ♣ A K J 10
♠ 9 8 6 5 3   ┌─────────┐   ♠ K J 7
♡ 10 9        │    N    │   ♡ K Q J
◇ K 4 3 2     │ W     E │   ◇ Q J 8 5
♣ 5 4         │    S    │   ♣ 9 3 2
              └─────────┘
              ♠ A 4 2
              ♡ A 8 7 6 5
              ◇ A
              ♣ Q 8 7 6
```

West	North	East	South
			1♡
pass	2♣	pass	3♣
pass	3♡	pass	4♡
all pass			

Opening lead: ♡ 10

After a duplicate event, the talk in the club lounge turned to this deal. Every North-South pair had reached four hearts.

'When I was South, the opening lead was a spade,' Cy the Cynic offered. 'I won, returned a spade and later ruffed a spade in dummy to take ten tricks.'

'Good for you,' Unlucky Louie grumbled. 'Against me they found the killing opening lead: a trump. I took the ace and led a spade, but the man won and cashed the K-Q of trumps. I lost another spade and went down.'

'You think a trump lead was the killer?' I asked. Louie eyed me warily.

'At the table I watched,' I said, 'South took the second trump and cashed the ace of diamonds. He got to dummy three times with clubs to ruff diamonds, then led a fourth club. East refused to ruff; but South next led dummy's last trump, and East had to lead from the king of spades.'

Tough game, bridge. With a spade lead South takes ten tricks; the 'killing' trump lead gives him a chance for eleven.

Bidding Quiz

YOU HOLD: ♠ A 4 2 ♡ A 8 7 6 5 ◇ A ♣ Q 8 7 6. Your partner opens one diamond, you respond one heart and he then bids one spade. The opponents pass. What do you say?

ANSWER: You could roar into 3NT, but you have time for investigation. Bid two clubs. Since you haven't yet passed, this bid of a new suit is forcing. If partner bids two diamonds or 2NT next, you can try 3NT, but if he bids two hearts, you'll bid four hearts.

Even Disposition

North dealer
Both vulnerable

```
                          ♠ Q 9 6 4 3
                          ♡ —
                          ◇ A 7 6 5
                          ♣ K 9 8 7
        ♠ K J                              ♠ 2
        ♡ K Q J 10 2          N            ♡ 9 8 7 6 5 4
        ◇ Q 8 3          W         E       ◇ 10 9 4
        ♣ Q 10 2             S            ♣ 5 4 3
                          ♠ A 10 8 7 5
                          ♡ A 3
                          ◇ K J 2
                          ♣ A J 6
```

West	North	East	South
	pass	pass	1♠
2♡	3♡	pass	4♣
pass	4◇	pass	5♠
pass	6♠	all pass	

Opening lead: ♡K

'I cut Grapefruit at rubber bridge today,' Ed (the best player in our club) told me. As I have mentioned, Grapefruit has a perfectly even disposition: always sour.

'On the first deal,' Ed related, 'he bid like a madman, and I was lucky to go down only one. Grapefruit growled that I could've made the hand three different ways. This was the next deal.'

Ed showed me the layout. 'I ruffed the first heart in dummy and led a trump to my ace. Next I led the ace of hearts and `absent-mindedly' ruffed it.'

'What did Grapefruit say to that?' I asked.

'Nothing I'd repeat,' Ed said. 'When I led a trump next, West was endplayed. If he led a minor, I'd get four tricks there; if he led a heart, I'd ruff in dummy, pitch a club, take the top clubs, ruff a club and throw a diamond on dummy's last club.'

'If you discard on the ace of hearts,' I said, 'you can't make it. Well done!'

'Grapefruit didn't think so,' Ed sighed. 'He muttered that God must look out for fools and his partners.'

Bidding Quiz

YOU HOLD: ♠ K J ♡ K Q J 10 2 ◇ Q 8 3 ♣ Q 10 2. You deal and open one heart, and your partner responds one spade. The opponents pass. What do you say?

ANSWER: Don't rebid two hearts, even though you have 100 honors, since you'd guarantee a six-card suit. You're never forced to rebid two hearts in this sequence with only five; you'll always have an alternative. Bid 1NT, promising 12 to 15 points with balanced distribution.

9. February 6   Harlow the Halo

West dealer
E-W vulnerable

```
              ♠ 4 3
              ♡ K J 6 5 2
              ◇ A Q J
              ♣ 6 4 2

              ♠ K Q J 10 9 6 2
              ♡ —
              ◇ K 10 9 3
              ♣ 7 3
```

West	North	East	South
1♣	1♡	2♣	4♠
dbl	all pass		

West leads the king of clubs and shifts to the six of diamonds. Plan the play.

10. February 10   Occupational Hazards

South dealer
N-S vulnerable

```
              ♠ 7 5 3
              ♡ 8 4
              ◇ K 4 3
              ♣ J 10 9 8 7

              ♠ A 8 4
              ♡ A Q J 10
              ◇ A Q 8 5
              ♣ A Q
```

West	North	East	South
			2NT
pass	3NT	all pass	

West leads the king of spades. You duck your ace twice and win the third spade as East follows. Plan the play.

11. February 12   That's Just Ducky

South dealer
E-W vulnerable

        ♠ Q J 5
        ♡ J 9 3 2
        ◊ 7 6 2
        ♣ A 6 4

        ♠ A 10 4
        ♡ Q 4
        ◊ A K Q 10 5
        ♣ K 5 2

West	North	East	South
			1◊
pass	1♡	pass	2NT
pass	3NT	all pass	

West leads the seven of clubs. Plan the play.

12. February 15   Louie's Good Fortune

South dealer
Neither vulnerable

        ♠ J 4
        ♡ A 9 3
        ◊ 7 6 5 4
        ♣ A 10 4 3

        ♠ A 7
        ♡ 7 6 5
        ◊ A K Q 2
        ♣ Q J 5 2

West	North	East	South
			1NT
pass	3NT	all pass	

West leads the deuce of spades: jack, queen from East. You take the ace, but when you cash the ◊ A-K, West discards a heart. Plan the play.

9. February 6

West dealer
E-W vulnerable

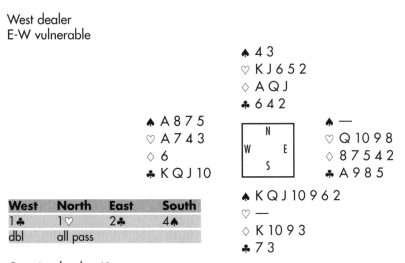

```
                      ♠ 4 3
                      ♡ K J 6 5 2
                      ◇ A Q J
                      ♣ 6 4 2
   ♠ A 8 7 5                          ♠ —
   ♡ A 7 4 3        ┌─────────┐       ♡ Q 10 9 8
   ◇ 6              │    N    │       ◇ 8 7 5 4 2
   ♣ K Q J 10       │ W     E │       ♣ A 9 8 5
                    │    S    │
                    └─────────┘
                      ♠ K Q J 10 9 6 2
                      ♡ —
                      ◇ K 10 9 3
                      ♣ 7 3
```

West	North	East	South
1♣	1♡	2♣	4♠
dbl	all pass		

Opening lead: ♣K

Success can be hard to handle, especially when it's somebody else's. Unlucky Louie is resigned to his bad luck, but it annoys him when the card gods favor a player we call Harlow the Halo. Harlow's luck is as good as Louie's is awful.

'The man could be looking for a needle in a haystack,' Louie grumbles, 'and he'd find not only the needle but the farmer's daughter.'

Both Louie and Harlow sat South in a duplicate game. When Louie played four spades doubled, West led his singleton diamond.

'It was a killer,' Louie told me. 'I won and led a trump, but West won and led the queen of clubs, deceiving East into winning with the ace and returning a diamond. West ruffed and cashed a club, and I was down with never a chance.

'Good defense,' I shrugged.

'The Halo also landed at four spades doubled,' Louie said, 'but West led the king of clubs and shifted to his singleton diamond. Harlow's no great declarer, but he won in dummy and led the king of hearts to discard his last club.'

'The good old Scissors Coup,' I noted.

'West won,' Louie nodded, 'but couldn't put East in with a club to get a ruff; so Harlow lost a trump, a heart and a club.'

The Halo was lucky indeed. West needed one trick from East to beat the contract. Since West had the ace of trumps and the ace of hearts, he knew South couldn't get fast discards for any losing clubs. West had no reason to lead anything at Trick 1 but his singleton to try for a ruff.

South dealer
N-S vulnerable

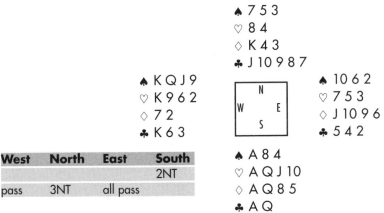

```
                        ♠ 7 5 3
                        ♡ 8 4
                        ◇ K 4 3
                        ♣ J 10 9 8 7
        ♠ K Q J 9              ♠ 10 6 2
        ♡ K 9 6 2      N       ♡ 7 5 3
        ◇ 7 2       W     E    ◇ J 10 9 6
        ♣ K 6 3         S      ♣ 5 4 2
                        ♠ A 8 4
                        ♡ A Q J 10
                        ◇ A Q 8 5
                        ♣ A Q
```

West	North	East	South
			2NT
pass	3NT	all pass	

Opening lead: ♠K

Cy the Cynic seems to have plenty of money, though where he got it is a mystery. The speculation about Cy's former occupation has developed into a running gag at the club that lets Cy's wit have full rein:

'Cy, were you a secretary?'

'No, I wasn't the type.'

'Were you a contortionist, Cy?'

'I couldn't make ends meet.'

'Did you work in a distillery?'

'Nope, they were only offering time and a fifth for overtime.'

'How about a chimney sweep?'

'It didn't soot me.'

Between fielding job queries, Cy was declarer at this 3NT contract, and afterwards it was in the same shape as his career as an archeologist: it lay in ruins. Cy won the third spade and led the ace and queen of clubs. West played low.

It wouldn't help Cy to lead to the king of diamonds and force out the king of clubs, since dummy would have no more entries. So Cy led a diamond to dummy and returned a heart to finesse. West took the king and cashed the king of clubs and his last spade to defeat the contract.

It's a good thing Cy doesn't have to make a living at bridge. How would you have played the hand?

After taking the ace of spades, South leads the queen of clubs without cashing the ace. West must play low, or else South can unblock the ace of clubs later and get to dummy with the king of diamonds for the clubs.

South next leads the ace and queen of hearts. West can win and cash his good spade, but South takes the rest, winning three hearts, three diamonds, two clubs and a spade.

South dealer
E-W vulnerable

```
                        ♠ Q J 5
                        ♡ J 9 3 2
                        ◇ 7 6 2
                        ♣ A 6 4
        ♠ K 9 8 6                        ♠ 7 3 2
        ♡ A 6 5          N              ♡ K 10 8 7
        ◇ 4         W         E         ◇ J 9 8 3
        ♣ Q 10 8 7 3        S           ♣ J 9
                        ♠ A 10 4
                        ♡ Q 4
                        ◇ A K Q 10 5
                        ♣ K 5 2
```

West	North	East	South
			1◇
pass	1♡	pass	2NT
pass	3NT	all pass	

Opening lead: ♣7

The fabulous Elfreda 'Ducky' van Tassel was at the club today. Depending on how the market closed, Ducky is either the richest person in town or close to it. If she lives to be 90, she won't have a party; she'll just split 3-for-1.

Ducky handles stock splits better than bad splits at bridge. As South, she won the first club in dummy and led the queen of spades to finesse. West played low, and Ducky next let the jack ride.

This time West won and led the queen of clubs. Ducky took the king, cashed the A-K of diamonds and sighed that diamonds weren't her best friend. East got the jack — Ducky couldn't get back to dummy to finesse — and the defense took the rest. Down two.

It's easy to handle the 4-1 diamond split. South can win the first club with the king and test diamonds by cashing the A-K. When West discards, South leads a low spade. Whatever West does, South gets to dummy to pick up the diamonds, winning five diamonds, two spades and two clubs.

Bidding Quiz

YOU HOLD: ♠ Q J 5 ♡ J 9 3 2 ◇ 7 6 2 ♣ A 6 4. Your partner opens one diamond, you respond one heart and he next bids two clubs. The opponents pass. What do you say?

ANSWER: Your partner surely has at least five diamonds; if he had four cards in each minor suit, he'd open one club. Bid two diamonds, returning to a suit in which you have eight trumps. Your hand is too weak for a more encouraging bid of 2NT, which would promise about 11 points.

12. February 15   Louie's Good Fortune

South dealer
Neither vulnerable

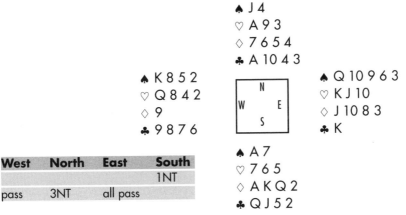

```
              ♠ J 4
              ♡ A 9 3
              ◇ 7 6 5 4
              ♣ A 10 4 3
♠ K 8 5 2              ♠ Q 10 9 6 3
♡ Q 8 4 2       N     ♡ K J 10
◇ 9        W       E  ◇ J 10 8 3
♣ 9 8 7 6       S     ♣ K
              ♠ A 7
              ♡ 7 6 5
              ◇ A K Q 2
              ♣ Q J 5 2
```

West	North	East	South
			1NT
pass	3NT	all pass	

Opening lead: ♠2

Some of us went to dinner at a Chinese restaurant, and Unlucky Louie's fortune cookie contained this: 'You will meet a beautiful woman; you will give her money.'

'Doesn't sound bad,' Louie smiled.

Louie also had high hopes later that evening at 3NT. He took the ace of spades and cashed the A-K of diamonds, scowling when West discarded a heart. Louie next let the queen of clubs ride, but East produced the king and cashed four spades. Down one.

'My luck is as bad as ever,' Louie sighed, 'but at least I'm going to meet a beautiful woman.'

'West's lead of the deuce marks him with four spades,' I said. 'After he shows up with a singleton diamond, he must have four hearts and four clubs or else he'd have held a five-card suit to lead from. If West has, say, K-9-8-7, you can never take four club tricks. Your only chance is to play East for the singleton king.'

Louie groaned.

'By the way,' I added, 'that cashier at the Chinese restaurant was a knockout, wasn't she?'

Bidding Quiz

YOU HOLD: ♠ J 4 ♡ A 9 3 ◇ 7 6 5 4 ♣ A 10 4 3. Your partner opens one spade, you respond 1NT and he rebids two spades. The opponents pass. What do you say?

ANSWER: Partner promises minimum values with at least six cards in spades. You have only 9 points, but since they consist of two aces and a 'working' jack, game is quite possible. Bid 2NT. If partner has a typical minimum such as ♠ A K Q 7 5 2 ♡ 6 4 ◇ J 3 2 ♣ K 6, 3NT will be a fine contract.

13. February 18 — Minnie's Big Gain

South dealer
Both vulnerable

```
                ♠ 6 4
                ♡ 7 6 3
                ◇ K J 5 2
                ♣ A Q J 5

                ♠ A 5
                ♡ A J 5
                ◇ A Q 8 6
                ♣ 10 9 7 4
```

West	North	East	South
			1NT
pass	3NT	all pass	

West leads the king of hearts. Plan the play.

14. February 23 — Thrown to the Lions

North dealer
Both vulnerable

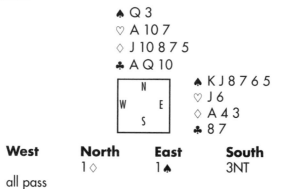

```
                ♠ Q 3
                ♡ A 10 7
                ◇ J 10 8 7 5
                ♣ A Q 10
                              ♠ K J 8 7 6 5
                              ♡ J 6
                              ◇ A 4 3
                              ♣ 8 7
```

West	North	East	South
	1◇	1♠	3NT
all pass			

West leads the four of spades, and dummy follows with the three. Plan the defense.

15. February 27 — Swept Away

West dealer
N-S vulnerable

```
                    ♠ Q J 9 7 3
                    ♡ A Q 6 4
                    ◊ 9 5
                    ♣ J 10
                    ┌─────────┐      ♠ 8 2
                    │    N    │      ♡ K 3
                    │ W     E │      ◊ K J 6 4
                    │    S    │      ♣ 9 7 6 4 3
                    └─────────┘
```

West	North	East	South
pass	pass	pass	1♡
pass	3♡	pass	6♡
all pass			

West leads the deuce of diamonds. Plan the defense.

16. March 1 — Overbid, Underplayed

South dealer
Both vulnerable

```
                    ♠ K J 6 4 3
                    ♡ J 5
                    ◊ A 8 7
                    ♣ A Q 3


                    ♠ A 2
                    ♡ A K 10
                    ◊ K Q 10
                    ♣ J 9 8 7 2
```

West	North	East	South
			1NT
pass	3♠	pass	3NT
pass	6NT	all pass	

West leads the nine of hearts. Plan the play.

Minnie's Big Gain

South dealer
Both vulnerable

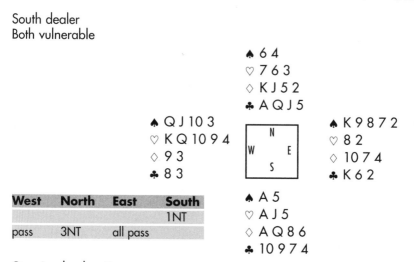

```
                    ♠ 6 4
                    ♡ 7 6 3
                    ♦ K J 5 2
                    ♣ A Q J 5
   ♠ Q J 10 3              ♠ K 9 8 7 2
   ♡ K Q 10 9 4      N     ♡ 8 2
   ♦ 9 3          W     E  ♦ 10 7 4
   ♣ 8 3             S     ♣ K 6 2
                    ♠ A 5
                    ♡ A J 5
                    ♦ A Q 8 6
                    ♣ 10 9 7 4
```

West	North	East	South
			1NT
pass	3NT	all pass	

Opening lead: ♡K

'I might have known.' Cy the Cynic was fuming over losing a match to a team captained by the dreaded Minnie Bottoms, our club's senior member. Minnie wears those ancient bifocals that make her get kings and jacks mixed up.

When Cy was declarer at 3NT, he refused the first heart, hoping West would lead another heart into the A-J. Instead, West shifted to the queen of spades. Cy won and finessed in clubs, but East won, and the defense ran the spades. Down two.

'I save one trick by winning the first heart,' Cy shrugged.

'What happened when Minnie played 3NT at the other table?' I asked.

'She neither won nor refused the first heart,' Cy said bitterly. 'Minnie played the jack! After my teammates convinced her that she hadn't won the trick, West continued hearts, of course.

'Minnie took the ace and lost a club finesse, but East had no more hearts. When he led a spade, Minnie took the ace and ran the clubs and diamonds for nine tricks and a big gain.'

Bidding Quiz

YOU HOLD: ♠ 6 4 ♡ 7 6 3 ♦ K J 5 2 ♣ A Q J 5. Your partner opens one spade, you respond two clubs, he bids two hearts and you try 2NT. Partner next bids three spades. What do you say?

ANSWER: Partner promises six spades, four hearts and extra strength. If he had minimum values, he'd have rebid two spades at his second turn to limit his strength. Raise to four spades or, if you're desperate to get your hands on the dummy, bid 3NT.

14. February 23 — Thrown to the Lions

North dealer
Both vulnerable

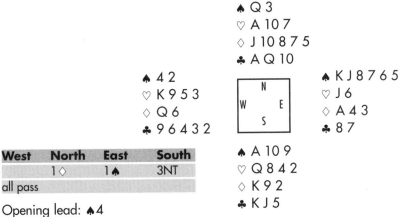

♠ Q 3
♡ A 10 7
◇ J 10 8 7 5
♣ A Q 10

♠ 4 2
♡ K 9 5 3
◇ Q 6
♣ 9 6 4 3 2

♠ K J 8 7 6 5
♡ J 6
◇ A 4 3
♣ 8 7

♠ A 10 9
♡ Q 8 4 2
◇ K 9 2
♣ K J 5

West	North	East	South
	1◇	1♠	3NT
all pass			

Opening lead: ♠4

One member of our club, Millard Pringle, is so polite I suspect he wouldn't even open an oyster without knocking. When Millard has the misfortune to cut the acid-tongued Grapefruit at rubber bridge, we all feel a good man is being thrown to the lions.

Grapefruit led a spade against 3NT after Millard's overcall. When dummy played low, Millard gulped, fumbled and produced the eight.

'Sorry,' he apologized. 'I'm not myself today.'

'Until now, I'd noticed the improvement,' snarled Grapefruit, always one to strike while the irony is hot.

South took the nine, led a club to dummy and let the jack of diamonds ride to the queen. On the next spade, Millard managed to cover the queen with the king. South won, but Millard won the next diamond and ran the spades. Down two. If Millard plays the jack on the first spade, South plays low, wins the next spade and finesses in diamonds. Since Grapefruit has no more spades, South then has time to set up the diamonds for nine tricks.

Bidding Quiz

YOU HOLD: ♠ Q 3 ♡ A 10 7 ◇ J 10 8 7 5 ♣ A Q 10. Your partner opens one spade, you bid two diamonds, he rebids two spades and you try 3NT. Partner then bids four hearts. What do you say?

ANSWER: Partner promises minimum values with six spades and four hearts. If he had five spades and four hearts (or extra strength), his second bid would have been two hearts. Bid four spades to play in the 6-2 spade fit rather than in the 4-3 heart fit.

West dealer
N-S vulnerable

```
                          ♠ Q J 9 7 3
                          ♡ A Q 6 4
                          ◊ 9 5
                          ♣ J 10
        ♠ 6 5 4                              ♠ 8 2
        ♡ 7 2                N              ♡ K 3
        ◊ 10 8 7 2       W       E          ◊ K J 6 4
        ♣ A 8 5 2            S              ♣ 9 7 6 4 3
                          ♠ A K 10
                          ♡ J 10 9 8 5
                          ◊ A Q 3
                          ♣ K Q
```

West	North	East	South
pass	pass	pass	1♡
pass	3♡	pass	6♡
all pass			

Opening lead: ◊ 2

Something had to give when our new member Wendy the Feminist cut Cy the Cynic at rubber bridge. Wendy can enjoy a man's company only if he owns it, while Cy swears some women think their work is done after they sweep down the aisle.

Cy, West, led the deuce of diamonds against South's slam, and Wendy's king lost to the ace. South then let the jack of trumps ride, and Wendy pounced with the king and almost split a fingernail returning a diamond. South produced the queen and claimed.

Wendy gave Cy a look that could have stuck four inches out of his back. 'Even a man should know to cash an ace against a slam — or to lead a higher diamond; the deuce promised an honor.'

'I had one,' Cy said shortly.

'Why didn't you tell Wendy it was all her fault?' I asked Cy later.

'You can't tell her anything,' Cy shrugged. 'She has a soundproof head.'

Wendy must play the jack on the first diamond. South is marked with the ace, but Wendy can find out who has the queen.

Bidding Quiz

YOU HOLD: ♠ A K 10 ♡ J 10 9 8 5 ◊ A Q 3 ♣ K Q. You open one heart, your partner responds one spade, you jump to 2NT and he next bids three clubs. The opponents pass. What do you say?

ANSWER: Bid four spades, promising strong three-card support. Partner almost surely has five cards in spades. If he's interested in slam, your jump will reassure him about the quality of your trumps. A bid of three spades would suggest a hand such as ♠ J 9 5 ♡ A K J 7 3 ◊ K 10 ♣ A Q 3.

16. March 1 — Overbid, Underplayed

South dealer
Both vulnerable

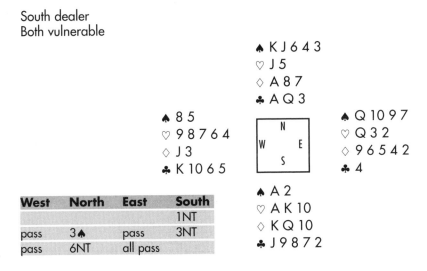

```
                    ♠ K J 6 4 3
                    ♡ J 5
                    ◇ A 8 7
                    ♣ A Q 3
    ♠ 8 5                        ♠ Q 10 9 7
    ♡ 9 8 7 6 4        N         ♡ Q 3 2
    ◇ J 3          W       E     ◇ 9 6 5 4 2
    ♣ K 10 6 5         S         ♣ 4
                    ♠ A 2
                    ♡ A K 10
                    ◇ K Q 10
                    ♣ J 9 8 7 2
```

West	North	East	South
			1NT
pass	3♠	pass	3NT
pass	6NT	all pass	

Opening lead: ♡9

When I watched this deal at the club, North was Will Rogers, who never met a hand he didn't like. Will never bothers with invitations: he figures if his partner lacks maximum values, the cards will lie well. Will had only 15 points and ragged spades for which South had denied help; still, he boomed into slam.

In fact, 6NT was a good spot, especially after West led a heart. But South was Joe Overberry, who plays every hand for the maximum — and often for the minimum. At Trick 2 Joe led a club to dummy's queen.

The finesse won, but then Joe took the ace of clubs. When East discarded, Joe still had a chance, but the spades treated him unkindly also. Down two.

'If the king of clubs falls, I make seven,' said Joe. Never mind that he'd given away 1540 points trying for an extra 30 points.

After the queen of clubs wins, South can play safe for four club tricks — all he needs. He returns to his hand, leads the seven of clubs and lets it ride if West plays low.

Bidding Quiz

YOU HOLD: ♠ K J 6 4 3 ♡ J 5 ◇ A 8 7 ♣ A Q 3. Dealer, on your right, opens one heart. You bid one spade, the next player raises to two hearts and two passes follow. What do you say?

ANSWER: Double. Since your partner hasn't acted, this double is for takeout. He'll support your spades or bid a minor suit. The bidding marks him with a few values, and your side probably has a fit since the opponents have found one. Hence you mustn't sell out cheaply.

17. March 6 — Money-Saving Defense

North dealer
Both vulnerable

```
                    ♠ K 3
                    ♡ 10 7 6
                    ◇ A K Q J
                    ♣ K Q 9 6

    ♠ A 7 4           N
    ♡ K 9 3 2      W     E
    ◇ 8 5             S
    ♣ A J 5 2
```

West	North	East	South
	1◇	pass	1♠
pass	2♣	pass	2♠
pass	4♠	all pass	

You lead the deuce of hearts. Declarer takes East's jack with the ace, leads a trump to the king and returns a trump to his queen, East following with the five and deuce. How do you defend?

18. March 9 — Louie's Misdefense

North dealer
Neither vulnerable

```
                    ♠ K 8 5
                    ♡ K 4 2
                    ◇ 6 2
                    ♣ A K 7 3 2

                    ♠ A Q 7 3 2
                    ♡ 7 3
                    ◇ A Q 4
                    ♣ Q 8 4
```

West	North	East	South
	1♣	pass	1♠
pass	2♠	pass	4♠
all pass			

West leads the queen of hearts. Plan the play.

19. March 12   Louie's Lovely Dream

South dealer
N-S vulnerable

```
              ♠ 10 6 4
              ♡ A 2
              ◇ A 10 9 8 5 2
              ♣ K 8

              ♠ Q J 8
              ♡ Q J 3
              ◇ K 7 4
              ♣ A J 9 4
```

West	North	East	South
			1♣
pass	1◇	1♡	1NT
pass	3NT	all pass	

West leads the seven of hearts. Plan the play.

20. March 14   A Cynical View

North dealer
N-S vulnerable

```
              ♠ Q J 4
              ♡ A 10 9
              ◇ J 7 4
              ♣ A K 9 5

              ♠ A 7 2
              ♡ Q 8 6
              ◇ Q 10 9 5
              ♣ Q J 7
```

West	North	East	South
	1♣	1♠	2NT
pass	3NT	all pass	

West leads the six of spades. Plan the play.

Money-Saving Defense

North dealer
Both vulnerable

```
                ♠ K 3
                ♡ 10 7 6
                ◇ A K Q J
                ♣ K Q 9 6
   ♠ A 7 4                      ♠ 6 5 2
   ♡ K 9 3 2        N           ♡ Q J 5 4
   ◇ 8 5        W       E       ◇ 10 9 6 2
   ♣ A J 5 2        S           ♣ 7 3
                ♠ Q J 10 9 8
                ♡ A 8
                ◇ 7 4 3
                ♣ 10 8 4
```

West	North	East	South
	1◇	pass	1♠
pass	2♣	pass	2♠
pass	4♠	all pass	

Opening lead: ♡2

The money games at my club range from a modest tenth of a cent a point to the 'big' ten-cent game. Still, few regulars make a living at the table: the competition is tough.

'I've tried to earn some money for a rainy day,' one would-be pro told me, 'but right now a heavy dew would clean me out. Look at this deal.'

South won the first heart and led a trump to dummy's king and a trump to West's ace. East echoed with the five and deuce, promising three trumps.

'If the defense cashes a heart and continues hearts,' South told me, 'I ruff, draw trumps and lead a club for ten tricks. But at Trick 4, West gave himself an extra chance: he shifted to the jack of clubs! Dummy won, but East signaled with the seven. When I led a heart next, West won, took the ace of clubs and gave East a club ruff.'

The deal came up in the big game, so West's defense saved his side a fortune. If East signals low on the jack of clubs, West will know he must try for two heart tricks.

Bidding Quiz

YOU HOLD: ♠ A 7 4 ♡ K 9 3 2 ◇ 8 5 ♣ A J 5 2. You open one club, your partner responds one diamond, you bid one heart and he then jumps to 2NT. The opponents pass. What do you say?

ANSWER: Your partner's second bid is, or should be, invitational to game, promising about 11 points, not forcing. If partner had 13 or more points, he could have jumped to 3NT or made a forcing bid. Since your opening bid contains not one bit of meat on the bones, pass.

18. March 9

North dealer
Neither vulnerable

```
              ♠ K 8 5
              ♡ K 4 2
              ◇ 6 2
              ♣ A K 7 3 2
    ♠ 6                      ♠ J 10 9 4
    ♡ Q J 10 9     N         ♡ A 8 6 5
    ◇ K J 10 8 7  W   E      ◇ 9 5 3
    ♣ J 10 5       S         ♣ 9 6
              ♠ A Q 7 3 2
              ♡ 7 3
              ◇ A Q 4
              ♣ Q 8 4
```

West	North	East	South
	1♣	pass	1♠
pass	2♠	pass	4♠
all pass			

Opening lead: ♡Q

'I know you think I bring it all on myself,' Unlucky Louie told me, 'but this was really-and-truly bad luck.'

'No doubt,' I said in the tone of polite disbelief I reserve for Louie's stories.

'I had the play planned right away,' Louie said. 'I'd ruff the third heart and cash the A-Q of trumps. If trumps broke 3-2, I'd draw the last trump and next play a low club from both hands, guarding against a 4-1 break. I'd be sure of five trumps, four clubs and a diamond.

'If trumps broke 4-1,' Louie went on, 'I'd shift to clubs after taking the A-Q. When a defender ruffed, I'd win the return, draw the last trump with the king and finish the clubs.'

'Seems foolproof,' I said.

'It wasn't,' Louie sighed. 'After West's queen of hearts won, for some reason he led the nine. I played low from dummy, but East was confused enough to take the ace! He then shifted to a diamond — and now try to make the contract.'

And I thought Louie's luck couldn't get any worse.

Bidding Quiz

YOU HOLD: ♠ K 8 5 ♡ K 4 2 ◇ 6 2 ♣ A K 7 3 2. You open one club, your partner responds one diamond and the next player bids one heart. What do you say?

ANSWER: Change your king of clubs to the queen and you'd pass to suggest a minimum hand. With your actual hand, bid 1NT freely. You have only 13 points, but a good five-card suit and a king of hearts that's worth more because it lies behind the opponent who overcalled.

19. March 12

South dealer
N-S vulnerable

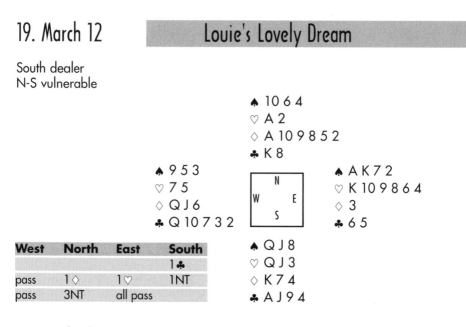

	♠ 10 6 4
	♡ A 2
	◇ A 10 9 8 5 2
	♣ K 8

♠ 9 5 3
♡ 7 5
◇ Q J 6
♣ Q 10 7 3 2

♠ A K 7 2
♡ K 10 9 8 6 4
◇ 3
♣ 6 5

♠ Q J 8
♡ Q J 3
◇ K 7 4
♣ A J 9 4

West	North	East	South
			1♣
pass	1◇	1♡	1NT
pass	3NT	all pass	

Opening lead: ♡7

I never expect to see Unlucky Louie make good on his threats to give up the game; he's a hopeless case.

'I had the loveliest dream last night,' he told me. 'I dreamed I talked Cindy Crawford into going to a tournament with me for a weekend.'

'Did your dream have a happy ending?' I asked.

'The best,' Louie gushed. 'Cindy and I won the Open Pairs.'

I think Louie was still dreaming when he was declarer in this deal. He played low from dummy on the first heart, and East took the king and led the deuce of spades. Louie won and tried the A-K of diamonds, but the deal became a nightmare when East showed out. West won the next diamond and led a spade, and East took three spades. Down one.

If Louie is awake, he'll grab the first heart with the ace, not giving East a chance for the deadly spade shift. Louie can then let the eight of diamonds ride as a safety play.

West wins, but Louie has eight tricks and plenty of time for another in hearts or spades to fulfill the contract.

Bidding Quiz

YOU HOLD: ♠ 10 6 4 ♡ A 2 ◇ A 10 9 8 5 2 ♣ K 8. Your partner opens one spade, you respond two diamonds and he then bids two hearts. The opponents pass. What do you say?

ANSWER: This decision is close. A bid of two spades would suggest invitational values; but since this hand contains prime honors and possible ruffing features in two suits, I'd insist on game. Jump to three spades (forcing after you've bid at the two-level originally).

20. March 14

North dealer
N-S vulnerable

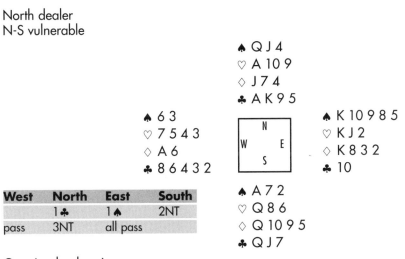

```
              ♠ Q J 4
              ♡ A 10 9
              ◇ J 7 4
              ♣ A K 9 5
 ♠ 6 3                        ♠ K 10 9 8 5
 ♡ 7 5 4 3      N            ♡ K J 2
 ◇ A 6      W       E        ◇ K 8 3 2
 ♣ 8 6 4 3 2      S          ♣ 10
              ♠ A 7 2
              ♡ Q 8 6
              ◇ Q 10 9 5
              ♣ Q J 7
```

West	North	East	South
	1♣	1♠	2NT
pass	3NT	all pass	

Opening lead: ♠6

Ask Cy the Cynic about the current state of bridge, and you'll get a cynical view: 'Most players are poor players,' Cy will say, 'including quite a few good players.'

East and South were good players but didn't perform like it. South put up dummy's queen on the first spade but refused the trick when East's king covered. South won the next spade with the jack and led a diamond.

West took the ace but had no more spades. When he led a heart, South rose with the ace, forced out the king of diamonds, and had four clubs, two diamonds, two spades and a heart.

East prevails if he doesn't cover the queen of spades. If dummy leads a diamond next, West can win and lead his last spade, setting up the spades while East still has the king of diamonds.

But South shouldn't give East a chance: on the first spade South must play low from dummy and his hand. When he wins the next spade, the defenders' link in spades is broken, and South has time to set up the diamonds.

Bidding Quiz

YOU HOLD: ♠ 6 3 ♡ 7 5 4 3 ◇ A 6 ♣ 8 6 4 3 2. Your partner opens two hearts (strong), you respond 2NT, he tries three diamonds and you jump to four hearts. Partner next bids four spades. The opponents pass. What do you say?

ANSWER: Your 2NT suggested weakness, and you bid four hearts because you did have four trumps and a useful ace. Partner knows your hand isn't robust but has still tried for slam. You owe him a cuebid of five diamonds.

21. March 18   Experience Preferred

North dealer
Neither vulnerable

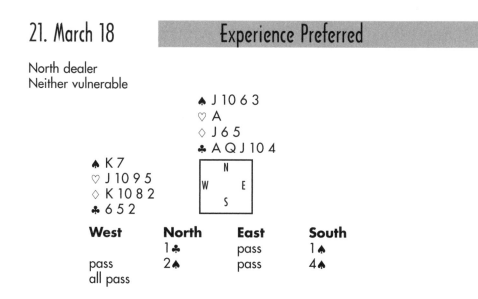

♠ J 10 6 3
♡ A
◊ J 6 5
♣ A Q J 10 4

♠ K 7
♡ J 10 9 5
◊ K 10 8 2
♣ 6 5 2

West	North	East	South
	1♣	pass	1♠
pass	2♠	pass	4♠
all pass			

You lead the jack of hearts. Declarer takes dummy's ace and passes the jack of spades to your king. What do you lead next?

22. March 20   Saving Partner

North dealer
N-S vulnerable

♠ Q J 10 5
♡ Q 9
◊ Q J 8
♣ A Q J 8

♠ 8
♡ K 5 2
◊ A K 10 4 2
♣ 10 7 6 2

West	North	East	South
	1♣	1◊	1♡
pass	1♠	pass	3♡
pass	4♡	all pass	

West leads the three of diamonds. Plan the defense.

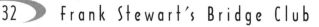

23. March 21   Louie's Emerald Day

South dealer
Neither vulnerable

```
          ♠ K 10 9 8 6
          ♡ A Q 7
          ◇ K Q 7
          ♣ 6 5

          ♠ Q J
          ♡ J 10 8
          ◇ A J 10 9
          ♣ K J 10 4
```

West	North	East	South
			1♣
pass	1♠	pass	1NT
pass	3NT	all pass	

West leads the six of hearts. Plan the play.

24. March 25   Just Showing Up

North dealer
N-S vulnerable

```
          ♠ —
          ♡ A Q 7 5
          ◇ J 8 7 6
          ♣ A K 7 4 3

          ♠ A 9 7
          ♡ 10 6 2
          ◇ Q 10 9 4 3 2
          ♣ 8
```

West	North	East	South
	1♣	dbl	1◇
pass	5◇	pass	pass
dbl	all pass		

West leads the four of hearts. Plan the play.

Experience Preferred

North dealer
Neither vulnerable

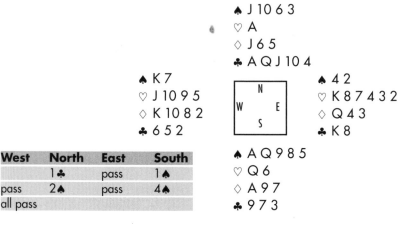

♠ J 10 6 3
♡ A
◇ J 6 5
♣ A Q J 10 4

♠ K 7
♡ J 10 9 5
◇ K 10 8 2
♣ 6 5 2

N
W   E
S

♠ 4 2
♡ K 8 7 4 3 2
◇ Q 4 3
♣ K 8

♠ A Q 9 8 5
♡ Q 6
◇ A 9 7
♣ 9 7 3

West	North	East	South
	1♣	pass	1♠
pass	2♠	pass	4♠
all pass			

Opening lead: ♡ J

'What's your definition of experience?' I asked some players at the club.

'It's what you get when you're expecting something else,' replied Cy the Cynic.

'What lets you recognize a mistake every time you repeat it,' Unlucky Louie offered.

West could have used a bit more experience in this deal. South let the jack of trumps ride at the second trick, and West won and shifted to the deuce of diamonds. South played low from dummy, took East's queen, drew trumps and lost a club finesse. East returned a diamond to West's king, and South claimed the rest, making his game.

A West who'd been around the block would lead the ten of diamonds at Trick 3 as an 'honor-trapping' play. If South covered with dummy's jack and took East's queen, East could get in with the king of clubs to return a diamond through South's 9-7 to West's K-8.

Experience may be what helps some people make old mistakes in new ways, but a winning player will learn from his mistakes.

Bidding Quiz

YOU HOLD: ♠ A Q 9 8 5 ♡ Q 6 ◇ A 9 7 ♣ 9 7 3. Your partner opens one heart, you respond one spade and he then bids 1NT. The opponents pass. What do you say?

ANSWER: Partner has a balanced 12 to 15 points. Since your hand is worth 13 points and your distribution is also balanced, bid 3NT. It's true partner may have three cards in spades, giving you an eight-card 'fit.' Still, you've no reason to think four spades would be a superior spot.

22. March 20 — Saving Partner

North dealer
N-S vulnerable

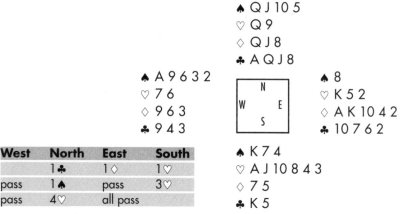

```
              ♠ Q J 10 5
              ♡ Q 9
              ◇ Q J 8
              ♣ A Q J 8
♠ A 9 6 3 2              ♠ 8
♡ 7 6         N          ♡ K 5 2
◇ 9 6 3    W     E       ◇ A K 10 4 2
♣ 9 4 3       S          ♣ 10 7 6 2
              ♠ K 7 4
              ♡ A J 10 8 4 3
              ◇ 7 5
              ♣ K 5
```

West	North	East	South
	1♣	1◇	1♡
pass	1♠	pass	3♡
pass	4♡	all pass	

Opening lead: ◇3

Cy the Cynic has gone through dozens of 'regular' partnerships. He defines a partner as someone who sticks by you through troubles you wouldn't have if your partner were someone else.

Today's North was strangely reluctant to bid notrump: he could have opened 1NT or tried 3NT over South's invitational three hearts. Game in notrump would succeed easily, but against four hearts, Cy, sitting West, led a diamond. East took dummy's jack with the king and returned the eight of spades to Cy's ace.

'I knew he might have led a singleton spade,' Cy told me, 'but what if he'd led from a doubleton? From his viewpoint, I might hold the king of spades instead of the ace, and he might need to set up a spade trick before declarer used dummy's clubs for a discard.'

I nodded agreement.

'So I returned a diamond to get our second diamond trick,' Cy went on. 'We got it, but declarer took the rest, drawing trumps with a finesse. My partner was ready to kill me for not giving him his ruff.'

I sympathized with Cy. It's easy to construct a deal in which East must lead a spade at Trick 2 (from any holding) to win a spade, two diamonds and a trump trick. Moreover, East could make the defense easy by winning the first diamond with the ace and leading a spade. Since East's play of the ace of diamonds would have seemed to deny possession of the king, Cy would have no choice but to take the ace of spades and return a spade, hoping East would ruff.

Louie's Emerald Day

South dealer
Neither vulnerable

```
                      ♠ K 10 9 8 6
                      ♡ A Q 7
                      ◇ K Q 7
                      ♣ 6 5
      ♠ 7 4 3                         ♠ A 5 2
      ♡ 6 4              N            ♡ K 9 5 3 2
      ◇ 8 5 4 3      W       E        ◇ 6 2
      ♣ A Q 7 3          S            ♣ 9 8 2
                      ♠ Q J
                      ♡ J 10 8
                      ◇ A J 10 9
                      ♣ K J 10 4
```

West	North	East	South
			1♣
pass	1♠	pass	1NT
pass	3NT	all pass	

Opening lead: ♡6

Unlucky Louie was at the club, accepting congratulations on his twentieth wedding anniversary.

'But last week I heard you say you and your wife were drifting apart,' I told him.

'We were,' Louie said blandly. 'We bought a used waterbed, and it sprang a leak.'

Later I watched Louie try to handle 3NT. He played low from dummy on the first heart, and East took the king and shifted to the nine of clubs: ten, queen. West returned a low club, and East's eight forced Louie's jack. When East got in with the ace of spades, he led another club, and West took the seven and ace. Down one!

According to Louie, one's twentieth anniversary is awkward: it's too soon to brag but too late to complain. In this deal, it was too late for him to either brag or complain after he ducked the opening lead.

Louie must instead grab the ace of hearts and force out the ace of spades. He is sure of four spades, four diamonds and one heart, and can lose no more than two clubs, a spade and a heart.

Bidding Quiz

YOU HOLD: ♠ K 10 9 8 6 ♡ A Q 7 ◇ K Q 7 ♣ 6 5. You open one spade, your partner responds two hearts, you raise to three hearts and he next bids four diamonds. The opponents pass. What do you say?

ANSWER: Partner's four diamonds is a cuebid to try for slam and promises the ace. You have no side ace to cuebid in return, but since you have good trumps and two helping diamond honors, your hand is too promising to sign off in four hearts. Bid five diamonds.

24. March 25

North dealer
N-S vulnerable

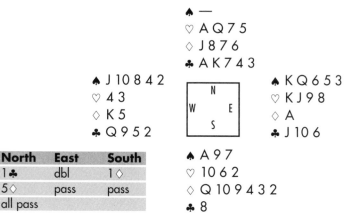

```
              ♠ —
              ♡ A Q 7 5
              ◇ J 8 7 6
              ♣ A K 7 4 3

  ♠ J 10 8 4 2           N        ♠ K Q 6 5 3
  ♡ 4 3              W        E    ♡ K J 9 8
  ◇ K 5                  S        ◇ A
  ♣ Q 9 5 2                        ♣ J 10 6

              ♠ A 9 7
              ♡ 10 6 2
              ◇ Q 10 9 4 3 2
              ♣ 8
```

West	North	East	South
	1♣	dbl	1◇
pass	5◇	pass	pass
dbl	all pass		

Opening lead: ♡4

'Those health spas are a ripoff,' Cy the Cynic grumbled. 'I joined one. They guaranteed I'd lose weight, and I haven't lost a pound.'

I knew Cy had scarcely left the bridge club for days.

'It might help if you went over there occasionally,' I suggested.

'You mean you have to show up?' Cy asked incredulously.

Cy played today's deal the same way, as if he expected eleven tricks to fall into his lap; he finessed with the queen on the first heart. East won, and Cy still had two trumps to lose.

East was likely to have the king of hearts, but Cy can succeed if he's willing to make the effort. He takes the ace of hearts, pitches a heart on the top clubs, ruffs a club, ruffs a spade, ruffs another club and ruffs a spade.

Cy then leads dummy's good club. If East ruffs with the ace, Cy discards his last heart and loses a trump to West's king. If instead East discards on the fifth club, Cy throws a heart. West ruffs low, but Cy later leads a trump to crash the defenders' A-K.

Bidding Quiz

YOU HOLD: ♠ — ♡ A Q 7 5 ◇ J 8 7 6 ♣ A K 7 4 3. Your partner opens one heart, and the next player bids one spade. What do you say?

ANSWER: Cuebid two spades, promising good heart support and a 'control' in spades: usually the ace or a void. You wouldn't cuebid if you weren't sure hearts will be trumps; but since a suitable minimum from your partner such as ♠ 7 6 4 ♡ K J 10 6 4 ◇ A K 2 ♣ Q 5 will yield a play for thirteen tricks, you should tell him now that slam is possible.

PART 2

Spring

1. March 28

South dealer
Both vulnerable

♠ Q 7 5
♡ 8 6 5
◇ 10 4 2
♣ K 7 5 2

♠ K J
♡ A 10 2
◇ A 9 6 5 3
♣ A 6 3

West	North	East	South
			1NT
all pass			

West leads the ten of spades, and your jack wins. How do you continue?

2. March 30

North dealer
Both vulnerable

♠ A Q J 10 9
♡ Q 3
◇ A J 7 3
♣ 10 2

♠ 7
♡ A 5
◇ K Q 10 9 6 5
♣ A Q J 9

West	North	East	South
	1♠	pass	2◇
pass	3◇	pass	4NT
pass	5♡	pass	5NT
pass	6♣	pass	6◇
all pass			

West leads the jack of hearts: queen, king, ace. How do you continue?

3. April 3

North dealer
Both vulnerable

♠ 7 6 3
♥ A 5
♦ A K 9 8 6
♣ J 8 4

♠ A K 9 8 4
♥ 9 7 4
♦ Q 3
♣ K 5 2

West	North	East	South
	1♦	pass	1♠
pass	1NT	pass	3♣
pass	3♠	pass	4♠
all pass			

West leads the queen of hearts. Plan the play.

4. April 5

Louie's Hefty Profit

South dealer
Both vulnerable

♠ 5 4 2
♥ 6 5 2
♦ 8 5 4 2
♣ J 7 3

♠ A K J 3
♥ A K Q J 10
♦ A K
♣ A K

West	North	East	South
			2♣
pass	2♦	pass	2♥
pass	2NT	pass	3♠
pass	4♥	pass	6♥
all pass			

West leads the jack of diamonds. Plan the play.

Going to the Dogs

South dealer
Both vulnerable

```
              ♠ Q 7 5
              ♡ 8 6 5
              ◇ 10 4 2
              ♣ K 7 5 2
♠ 10 9 8                    ♠ A 6 4 3 2
♡ Q J 4           N         ♡ K 9 7 3
◇ K J 8 7      W     E      ◇ Q
♣ Q 10 9          S         ♣ J 8 4
              ♠ K J
              ♡ A 10 2
              ◇ A 9 6 5 3
              ♣ A 6 3
```

West	North	East	South
			1NT
all pass			

Opening lead: ♠ 10

'I thought I had a problem today,' a player told me as we awaited the results of an afternoon duplicate.

'Can I help?'

'Not quite,' she said. 'My husband came in hungry from his morning golf game, headed for the refrigerator and gulped down some dog food I was saving for our beagle. I thought I'd better not tell him what he'd done, but midway through the bridge game he started to scratch himself and then he misplayed this hand.

'He won the first spade with the jack and led a diamond to dummy's ten. East won and returned a low spade. My husband then led the ace of diamonds, and East showed out. My hubby took only six tricks.'

'He didn't need to duck the first diamond,' I said. 'He had plenty of entries to his hand. If he leads the ace first, he's home.'

'He was also complaining of a headache,' she said. 'To be safe, I called our doctor.'

'What'd he say?'

'He didn't sound worried. He said if my husband started chasing cars, to bring him in.'

Bidding Quiz

YOU HOLD: ♠ 10 9 8 ♡ Q J 4 ◇ K J 8 7 ♣ Q 10 9. Dealer, on your left, opens one diamond. Your partner doubles, you respond 1NT and partner raises to 2NT. The opponents pass. What do you say?

ANSWER: Your bid of 1NT promised 6 to 9 points with balanced distribution and a trick or two in diamonds. Your hand is really a super-maximum, since you have good intermediate cards as well as 9 points in high cards. Bid 3NT.

North dealer
Both vulnerable

```
                        ♠ A Q J 10 9
                        ♡ Q 3
                        ◇ A J 7 3
                        ♣ 10 2
        ♠ 5 3 2                         ♠ K 8 6 4
        ♡ J 10 9 8 4          N         ♡ K 7 6 2
        ◇ 8 2             W       E     ◇ 4
        ♣ K 7 6               S         ♣ 8 5 4 3
                        ♠ 7
                        ♡ A 5
                        ◇ K Q 10 9 6 5
                        ♣ A Q J 9
```

West	North	East	South
	1♠	pass	2◇
pass	3◇	pass	4NT
pass	5♡	pass	5NT
pass	6♣	pass	6◇
all pass			

Opening lead: ♡J

Unlucky Louie had suffered the ultimate disaster: a restaurant had inadvertently switched his credit card with someone else's.

'My account's a mess,' Louie moaned. 'I'm so far in debt you could call me a collector's item.'

'Your best chance is to move away and start a new life under an assumed name,' I told him cheerfully.

In the problem deal, Louie covered the jack of hearts with dummy's queen and took East's king. Louie then drew trumps and let the ten of clubs ride. West won and cashed a heart, pushing Louie a little deeper into the hole.

Louie's line of play was even worse than his line of credit. He can take the cash and let the credit go if he leads the ace and then the queen of spades after drawing trumps, intending to pitch his losing heart if East plays low.

As the cards lie, Louie loses one club trick; but even if East took the king of spades, Louie could ruff the heart return, lead a trump to dummy and discard three clubs on the good spades.

Bidding Quiz

YOU HOLD: ♠ 7 ♡ A 5 ◇ K Q 10 9 6 5 ♣ A Q J 9. You open one diamond, and your partner bids one spade. The opponents pass. What do you say?

ANSWER: A jump to three diamonds, promising 16 to 18 points with six good diamonds, is possible, but a bid of two clubs is more flexible. You plan to bid three diamonds next, suggesting six diamonds, four clubs and extra strength, but if partner passes two clubs, it may even be your best spot.

3. April 3

North dealer
Both vulnerable

```
                    ♠ 7 6 3
                    ♡ A 5
                    ◇ A K 9 8 6
                    ♣ J 8 4
      ♠ J 2                        ♠ Q 10 5
      ♡ Q J 10 3 2      N          ♡ K 8 6
      ◇ 7 4         W       E      ◇ J 10 5 2
      ♣ A 10 9 3        S          ♣ Q 7 6
                    ♠ A K 9 8 4
                    ♡ 9 7 4
                    ◇ Q 3
                    ♣ K 5 2
```

West	North	East	South
	1◇	pass	1♠
pass	1NT	pass	3♣
pass	3♠	pass	4♠
all pass			

Opening lead: ♡Q

My English professor friend must be finding his retirement restless; he comes to the bridge club almost every day.

'Hear about the prison inmate,' he asked me, 'who was told he'd get an early release if he came on to the warden's wife?'

'Did he?'

'No,' said the prof blandly. 'He didn't want to end his sentence with a proposition.'

After which awful joke, the prof watched South play four spades. South won the first heart and returned a heart, and East won and led a third heart, forcing dummy to ruff. South next took the A-K of trumps and cashed three diamonds to throw a club. When West discarded, South had to try a club to the king next, and down he went, losing two clubs and a trump.

'The sort of dummy play up with which I will not put,' the prof growled. 'Refuse the first heart! If West leads another heart, you cash the top trumps and then three diamonds, throwing a club. You then ruff a diamond, get back with a heart ruff and throw another club on the fifth diamond, assuring the contract.'

Bidding Quiz

YOU HOLD: ♠ J 2 ♡ Q J 10 3 2 ◇ 7 4 ♣ A 10 9 3. Your partner opens one spade, you respond 1NT and he then bids two hearts. The opponents pass. What do you say?

ANSWER: What began as a hand worth little more than 8 points has blossomed. Every honor will be useful to partner, and your fifth card in hearts will make it easier for him to set up his spades. Since many minimum opening bids for partner will make game, bid four hearts.

4. April 5

South dealer
Both vulnerable

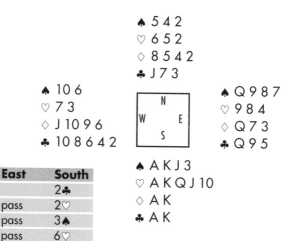

```
                    ♠ 5 4 2
                    ♡ 6 5 2
                    ◇ 8 5 4 2
                    ♣ J 7 3
    ♠ 10 6                          ♠ Q 9 8 7
    ♡ 7 3              N            ♡ 9 8 4
    ◇ J 10 9 6    W        E        ◇ Q 7 3
    ♣ 10 8 6 4 2       S            ♣ Q 9 5
                    ♠ A K J 3
                    ♡ A K Q J 10
                    ◇ A K
                    ♣ A K
```

West	North	East	South
			2♣
pass	2◇	pass	2♡
pass	2NT	pass	3♠
pass	4♡	pass	6♡
all pass			

Opening lead: ◇ J

'I picked up one of my usual,' Unlucky Louie told me in the lounge, 'with one jack. I was sure the rubber had gone west; but then partner bid a slam with no particular encouragement.'

'He must have had a whale,' I surmised.

'He'd have needed Moby Dick's big brother to make six hearts opposite my hand,' Louie said.

Louie's partner won the first diamond and drew trumps. He cashed a fourth trump for exercise and next led the ace, king and a low spade. East took the nine and queen, defeating the slam.

'He had 32 high-card points,' Louie said, 'and we made a big 50-point profit thanks to his 150 honors.'

'If you'd been South, you'd have made the slam,' I said. 'You'd lead a low spade at Trick 2. When you got back in, you'd cash two trumps and then the A-K of spades. You're safe if the queen falls or, as in the actual deal, if a defender with four spades also has the last missing trump. Too bad you were sitting in the wrong seat.'

'I always am,' Louie sighed.

Bidding Quiz

YOU HOLD: ♠ Q 9 8 7 ♡ 9 8 4 ◇ Q 7 3 ♣ Q 9 5. Your partner opens two clubs (strong and forcing), you bid a negative two diamonds, and partner rebids two spades. What do you say?

ANSWER: This is a textbook situation. Raise to four spades, promising good trump support but denying any side ace, king, void or singleton. Your partner will often stop at game, but if all he needs from you to make a slam is a stray queen or two, he'll bid again.

5. April 9

South dealer
Neither vulnerable

    ♠ 10 7 4
    ♡ K J 9
    ◇ J 8 7 4
    ♣ 10 6 2

    ♠ A K Q J 5
    ♡ A Q 8 5
    ◇ A 6
    ♣ Q 3

West	North	East	South
			1♠
pass	1NT	pass	3♡
pass	3♠	pass	3NT
pass	4♠	all pass	

West leads the king of clubs and continues with the ace and jack. East follows. Plan the play.

6. April 12

North dealer
Neither vulnerable

    ♠ A 8 4 2
    ♡ Q 9 8
    ◇ 10 5 2
    ♣ K 8 3

    ♠ 7 5
    ♡ A J 10 7 4 2
    ◇ A K J 4
    ♣ 6

West	North	East	South
	pass	3♣	3♡
pass	4♡	all pass	

West leads the king of spades. You take the ace and let the queen of trumps ride. West wins and cashes the queen of spades, and East shows out. West then shifts to the jack of clubs and another club. You ruff. How do you continue?

7. April 16

South dealer
Both vulnerable

♠ A Q 5 3
♥ 4
♦ 10 7 6 2
♣ J 6 5 3

♠ 4
♥ A K J 10 9 8 7
♦ A Q J
♣ K 8

West	North	East	South
			1 ♥
pass	1 ♠	pass	4 ♥
all pass			

West leads the ten of spades. Plan the play.

8. April 19

South dealer
E-W vulnerable

♠ 8 5
♥ A 2
♦ A J 9 8 6 4
♣ K 9 4

♠ K 9 6 3
♥ 10
♦ Q 5
♣ A Q J 10 7 6

West	North	East	South
			1 ♣
1 ♥	2 ♦	2 ♥	3 ♣
pass	5 ♣	all pass	

West leads the king of hearts. Plan the play.

South dealer
Neither vulnerable

```
                      ♠ 10 7 4
                      ♡ K J 9
                      ♢ J 8 7 4
                      ♣ 10 6 2
  ♠ 9 8 6 3 2                        ♠ —
  ♡ 7               N                ♡ 10 6 4 3 2
  ♢ 5 2          W     E             ♢ K Q 10 9 3
  ♣ A K J 9 4       S                ♣ 8 7 5
                      ♠ A K Q J 5
                      ♡ A Q 8 5
                      ♢ A 6
                      ♣ Q 3
```

West	North	East	South
			1♠
pass	1NT	pass	3♡
pass	3♠	pass	3NT
pass	4♠	all pass	

Opening lead: ♣K

'What's the chance of a 5-0 break anyway?' Unlucky Louie demanded after this deal. 'For the rest of the world, I mean, not for me.'

I knew the odds. 'A suit will break 5-0 about 4 percent of the time,' I answered, 'though for you, the chances may be more in the neighborhood of 50-50.'

West took the king and ace of clubs and continued with the jack. Louie ruffed and cashed the ace of trumps, squirming when East discarded a diamond. Louie then drew three more trumps and started the hearts, but West ruffed the second heart and cashed two more clubs, defeating the contract.

'For most players, the chances of making it were 96 percent,' Louie grumbled, 'and even I, the accursed one, had an even chance.'

'Actually, the chances for a careful player are about 100 percent,' I informed him. 'Instead of ruffing the third club, pitch your losing diamond. You win the next trick, draw trumps — in five rounds if necessary — and claim.'

And Louie turned as purple as a grape.

Bidding Quiz

YOU HOLD: ♠ 9 8 6 3 2 ♡ 7 ♢ 5 2 ♣ A K J 9 4. Your partner opens one spade, and the next player passes. What do you say?

ANSWER: Although you have five trumps and good distribution, this hand has too much slam potential for a leap to four spades. Many minimum hands for partner — for example, five spades to the A-K, the ace of diamonds and the queen of clubs — would produce twelve tricks. Bid two clubs and jump to three spades or four spades next.

6. April 12

North dealer
Neither vulnerable

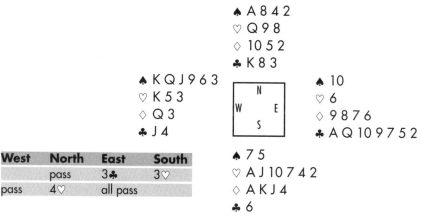

♠ A 8 4 2
♡ Q 9 8
♢ 10 5 2
♣ K 8 3

♠ K Q J 9 6 3
♡ K 5 3
♢ Q 3
♣ J 4

♠ 10
♡ 6
♢ 9 8 7 6
♣ A Q 10 9 7 5 2

♠ 7 5
♡ A J 10 7 4 2
♢ A K J 4
♣ 6

West	North	East	South
	pass	3♣	3♡
pass	4♡	all pass	

Opening lead: ♠K

'You know,' Unlucky Louie told me, 'some hands you just have to play on faith.'

'Did I ever tell you about the time I applied for a job as a faith healer?' Cy the Cynic piped up.

'Were you hired?' Louie asked.

'No,' Cy said solemnly, 'they said I lacked hands-on experience.'

Louie groaned and displayed this deal. 'I took the ace of spades and lost the trump finesse. West cashed a spade and shifted to clubs. I ruffed the second club, led a trump to dummy, ruffed a club and took the queen of trumps. By then I knew West had started with six spades, three hearts and two clubs — so two diamonds.

'A finesse with the jack wouldn't help: even if East had the queen, he'd get a diamond. My only chance was to take the A-K, hoping West had the doubleton queen.'

'Well done,' I said.

'I thought so,' Louie sighed, 'but West claimed I was lucky — which really rubbed me the wrong way.'

'I once lost a job as a masseur because I did that to too many people,' mumbled the Cynic.

Bidding Quiz

YOU HOLD: ♠ 7 5 ♡ A J 10 7 4 2 ♢ A K J 4 ♣ 6. Your partner opens one diamond, and the next player passes. What do you say?

ANSWER: A grand slam is likely if partner has the right 13 points -- the black aces, the queen of diamonds and the king of hearts — and he promises 13 or more. Jump to two hearts to show slam interest and support the diamonds next. If you bid one heart, it'll be hard to get partner to cooperate in a slam hunt.

South dealer
Both vulnerable

```
                        ♠ A Q 5 3
                        ♡ 4
                        ◇ 10 7 6 2
                        ♣ J 6 5 3
        ♠ 10 9 8 7                      ♠ K J 6 2
        ♡ 6                 N            ♡ Q 5 3 2
        ◇ 9 5 3          W     E         ◇ K 8 4
        ♣ Q 10 7 4 2        S            ♣ A 9
                        ♠ 4
                        ♡ A K J 10 9 8 7
                        ◇ A Q J
                        ♣ K 8
```

West	North	East	South
			1♡
pass	1♠	pass	4♡
all pass			

Opening lead: ♠10

It was supposed to be a sun-washed day; instead, raindrops were doing needlepoint on the bridge club's roof.

'If Noah had consulted a weatherman,' one player observed as he stared out a window, 'there'd have been a 20 percent chance of his building the Ark.'

Since bridge isn't an outdoor sport, the game went on, and South arrived at four hearts. He took the ace of spades, wondered which finesse to try and eventually led a diamond to his jack, winning.

South next cashed the A-K of trumps and led the jack. East took the queen and got out with his last trump, and South then took the ace of diamonds and led the queen. East won and led the king of spades, and South ruffed and had to lead a club from his hand, losing two clubs. Down one.

South's play was all wet just like the roof. Even if he wins a diamond or a trump finesse, he may lose a trick in that suit. South should instead try a finesse that's sure to gain if it wins: he should lead a club to his king at Trick 2.

Bidding Quiz

YOU HOLD: ♠ K J 6 2 ♡ Q 5 3 2 ◇ K 8 4 ♣ A 9. You are the dealer with neither vulnerable. What do you say?

ANSWER: Bid one diamond. It's unpleasant to open a three-card suit, but the alternative — to open a ragged four-card major suit — is worse. You hope partner will respond in a major, but if he raises to two diamonds, you'll pass. Don't even think of opening one club on a two-card suit; that way madness lies.

8. April 19

South dealer
E-W vulnerable

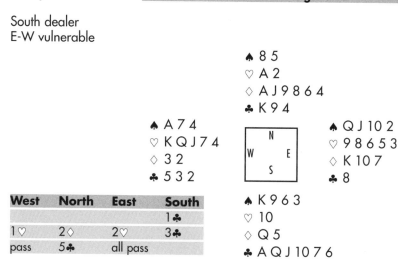

♠ 8 5
♡ A 2
♢ A J 9 8 6 4
♣ K 9 4

♠ A 7 4
♡ K Q J 7 4
♢ 3 2
♣ 5 3 2

♠ Q J 10 2
♡ 9 8 6 5 3
♢ K 10 7
♣ 8

♠ K 9 6 3
♡ 10
♢ Q 5
♣ A Q J 10 7 6

West	North	East	South
			1♣
1♡	2♢	2♡	3♣
pass	5♣	all pass	

Opening lead: ♡K

'Things have been so bad lately,' Unlucky Louie told me as he sat down to play in the half-cent Chicago game, 'that I need a rash of good luck.'

'Easy,' I remarked. 'Just cross a four-leaf clover with some poison ivy.'

Louie soon picked up the South hand and got to five clubs. He took the ace of hearts, led a trump to the hand and let the queen of diamonds ride. East took the king and led the queen of spades, and the defense got two spades. Down one.

'Same old story,' Louie growled. 'Two finesses out of two lose.'

I don't know about Louie's luck, but his judgment at Trick 1 was rash: he should let West's king of hearts win. If West leads another heart, Louie discards a diamond on the ace.

Louie can then set up the diamonds without letting East in for a spade shift: ace of diamonds, diamond ruff high, trump to dummy's nine, diamond ruff high. Louie then draws trumps with the ace and king and throws three spades on the good diamonds, losing only one heart and one spade.

Bidding Quiz

YOU HOLD: ♠ 8 5 ♡ A 2 ♢ A J 9 8 6 4 ♣ K 9 4. You open one diamond, your partner bids one spade, you rebid two diamonds and he tries 2NT. The opponents pass. What do you say?

ANSWER: Partner is inviting game; he has about 11 points with balanced distribution. You promised 12 to 15 points with a six-card diamond suit. You might take a shot at game if your jack of diamonds were the queen, but your actual hand is a bare minimum. Pass.

9. April 22   Charmed, I'm Sure

East dealer
N-S vulnerable

```
            ♠ J
            ♡ 10 8 7 6 3
            ◊ Q J 10 7
            ♣ A Q 6

            ♠ K Q 8 7 6 5 2
            ♡ A
            ◊ K
            ♣ K J 10 3
```

West	North	East	South
		1♡	1♠
pass	1NT	2♡	4♠
all pass			

West leads the deuce of hearts. You win and lead a trump, and East takes the ace and leads the king of hearts. How do you play?

10. April 25   Blackjack

East dealer
Both vulnerable

```
            ♠ 10 4 2
            ♡ 9 8 6 3
            ◊ 9 7 3
            ♣ 10 9 8

            ♠ A K Q J 3
            ♡ 7 5
            ◊ A Q 10
            ♣ A J 7
```

West	North	East	South
		1NT	dbl
2◊	pass	pass	4♠ (!)
all pass			

West leads the queen of hearts and continues with the jack and a third heart to East's king. Plan the play.

11. April 28 — That Kind of Day

South dealer
N-S vulnerable

♠ 9 8 6 5 2
♡ K Q 10
♢ 7 4 2
♣ A 4

♠ A Q
♡ A J 9 8 7 6
♢ A 8 3
♣ 10 2

West	North	East	South
			1♡
pass	2♡	pass	3♡
pass	4♡	all pass	

West leads the queen of diamonds. Plan the play.

12. May 2 — Overmatched

South dealer
Both vulnerable

♠ 8 7 6 2
♡ A J 8 3
♢ 8 7 3
♣ 7 4

♠ A K J 9 3
♡ 6
♢ J 10 5
♣ A K 10 6

West	North	East	South
			1♠
pass	2♠	pass	4♠
all pass			

West leads the four of hearts. Plan the play.

9. April 22

East dealer
N-S vulnerable

```
                              ♠ J
                              ♡ 10 8 7 6 3
                              ◇ Q J 10 7
                              ♣ A Q 6
        ♠ 10 9 4 3                          ♠ A
        ♡ 2                    N             ♡ K Q J 9 5 4
        ◇ 8 6 5 3 2        W       E         ◇ A 9 4
        ♣ 9 7 2               S             ♣ 8 5 4
                              ♠ K Q 8 7 6 5 2
                              ♡ A
                              ◇ K
                              ♣ K J 10 3
```

West	North	East	South
		1♡	1♠
pass	1NT	2♡	4♠
all pass			

Opening lead: ♡2

'Are you superstitious?' Cy the Cynic asked me.

'No,' I replied, 'and I thank my lucky stars I'm not.'

'Today,' Cy said, 'I partnered a guy who had a rabbit's foot around his neck and a horseshoe nailed to his chair.'

'Did they work?' I asked.

'You judge,' Cy replied. 'He took the ace of hearts and led a trump, and East won and led a high heart. My partner tossed some salt over his shoulder and ruffed with the eight. West overruffed and led a diamond, and East won and led another heart.

'My partner pulled out a four-leaf clover and ruffed with the king of trumps, but it didn't matter; he was sure to lose another trump trick to West and go down.

'The guy attributed his defeat to a black cat that had crossed his path,' Cy went on, 'but he's safe if he throws the king of diamonds on the second heart and ruffs the next heart low. West overruffs, but partner wins the rest.

'Anyway, I hope I never cut him as a partner again.'

'Knock on wood,' I nodded.

Bidding Quiz

YOU HOLD: ♠ A ♡ K Q J 9 5 4 ◇ A 9 4 ♣ 8 5 4. Your partner opens one spade, you respond two hearts and he raises to three hearts. The opponents pass. What do you say?

ANSWER: Partner may have minimum values, but a typical minimum hand for him such as ♠ K Q 9 5 2 ♡ A 8 6 3 ◇ 8 2 ♣ A 3 will produce twelve tricks. Cuebid four diamonds, showing the ace and slam interest. Even if partner signs off in four hearts, you'll try again by cuebidding four spades.

10. April 25

East dealer
Both vulnerable

```
                    ♠ 10 4 2
                    ♡ 9 8 6 3
                    ◊ 9 7 3
                    ♣ 10 9 8
        ♠ 8 6                      ♠ 9 7 5
        ♡ Q J 2          N         ♡ A K 10 4
        ◊ 8 6 5 4 2   W     E      ◊ K J
        ♣ 5 4 2          S         ♣ K Q 6 3
                    ♠ A K Q J 3
                    ♡ 7 5
                    ◊ A Q 10
                    ♣ A J 7
```

West	North	East	South
		1NT	dbl
2◊	pass	pass	4♠ (!)
all pass			

Opening lead: ♡Q

'See that fierce-looking guy sitting at the table in the corner?' a player at the club asked me, pointing to a man with a face as cratered as the moon and a mustache as big and dark as a Halloween hobgoblin. 'They tell me his name is Blackjack Barton. Was he a pro gambler or a dealer at a casino someplace?'

'No,' I said solemnly, 'but I think he once served as a mob enforcer.'

My friend's eyes widened.

I laughed. 'Just kidding. Blackjack's all right. He has a wife and kids.'

'How'd he get his nickname?'

'We think because of this deal,' I replied. 'It came up in a duplicate event long ago, and Blackjack was the only declarer to make four spades.

'The defense started with three rounds of hearts, and a few Souths foolishly ruffed with the three and drew trumps. Since they couldn't get to dummy, they had to lead both clubs and diamonds from their hand, losing as many as five tricks in all.

'Blackjack ruffed the third heart with the jack of spades — that was one black jack — and at Trick 2 he slid out another: the jack of clubs.

'East won and led another heart, but Blackjack ruffed high again and drew trumps with the ace, king and ten. He could then let the ten of clubs ride and finesse in diamonds next. When East's K-J of diamonds fell, Blackjack was home.

'He played it well,' my friend admitted, 'but his leap to game wouldn't occur to me.'

'Blackjack never stops below game when he has 21 points,' I smiled.

South dealer
N-S vulnerable

```
                        ♠ 9 8 6 5 2
                        ♡ K Q 10
                        ◇ 7 4 2
                        ♣ A 4
    ♠ K 4                                 ♠ J 10 7 3
    ♡ 5 4 3               N               ♡ 2
    ◇ Q J 10 9      W          E          ◇ K 6 5
    ♣ J 8 6 3               S            ♣ K Q 9 7 5
                        ♠ A Q
                        ♡ A J 9 8 7 6
                        ◇ A 8 3
                        ♣ 10 2
```

West	North	East	South
			1♡
pass	2♡	pass	3♡
pass	4♡	all pass	

Opening lead: ◇Q

Unlucky Louie was having the kind of day that should have quit while it was still morning. He was already deep in the hole when he heard North raise his one heart opening bid to two.

'I ought to pass,' Louie muttered. But he tried again with three hearts — what his cards were worth even after subtracting a point for bad luck. North bid game.

Louie won the first diamond, led a trump to dummy and returned a spade to the queen. West took the king, and the defense cashed two diamonds. East then led the king of clubs. Louie won, cashed the ace of spades, led a trump to dummy and ruffed a spade, hoping for a 3-3 break. When West discarded, Louie couldn't avoid losing a club. Down one.

'The only way I'd ever have a day when nothing went wrong,' Louie sighed, 'was if I were a repairman.'

Meanwhile, North unleashed some barbed ire. 'Bid 2NT over two hearts and I'll raise to 3NT,' he scowled. 'Not even you could go down there.' Louie said nothing, as a politician who wouldn't dignify some comments with a response.

Louie should make four hearts. After taking the ace of diamonds, he cashes the ace of trumps and leads the ace and queen of spades. The defense takes two diamonds and leads a club, but Louie wins, ruffs a spade, returns with the queen of trumps and ruffs a spade. He can then draw trumps with the king and pitch a club on the winning spade.

This line works when spades break no worse than 4-2: about 84 percent of the time. Louie's line wasn't as good.

12. May 2

South dealer
Both vulnerable

```
                        ♠ 8 7 6 2
                        ♡ A J 8 3
                        ◇ 8 7 3
                        ♣ 7 4
   ♠ Q 10 4                                ♠ 5
   ♡ Q 10 7 4 2          N                 ♡ K 9 5
   ◇ K 9 4          W         E            ◇ A Q 6 2
   ♣ Q 3                S                  ♣ J 9 8 5 2
                        ♠ A K J 9 3
                        ♡ 6
                        ◇ J 10 5
                        ♣ A K 10 6
```

West	North	East	South
			1♠
pass	2♠	pass	4♠
all pass			

Opening lead: ♡4

Ed, my club's best player, is so hard to beat that our members have begun to feel over-matched.

'He could follow me into a revolving door and come out ahead of me,' is how Cy the Cynic puts it.

Not even Ed would have made four spades if West had led a diamond; but when West led a heart, Ed took dummy's ace, thought for twenty seconds... and ruffed a heart! He next took the A-K of trumps. When East discarded, Ed led the A-K and a low club. If West ruffed in with the queen, dummy would discard a losing diamond, so West threw a heart, and dummy ruffed.

Ed then ruffed a heart and led his last club. West had to pitch a diamond, keeping the queen of hearts to beat dummy's jack, so Ed ruffed in dummy and ruffed the jack of hearts with his last trump for the tenth trick.

Most players would lead a trump at the second trick to take the A-K; they'd lose a trump and three diamonds. Unless South displays precise timing by ruffing a heart at Trick 2, down he goes.

Bidding Quiz

YOU HOLD: ♠ A K J 9 3 ♡ 6 ◇ J 10 5 ♣ A K 10 6. Your partner opens one club, and the next player passes. What do you say?

ANSWER: Bid two spades to put your partner in the picture. Slam chances are too bright not to let him know immediately with a jump. If partner has a suitable minimum hand such as ♠ Q 4 ♡ A 5 4 ◇ A 9 3 ♣ Q J 8 5 2 he'll easily take thirteen tricks in a club contract; but if you respond only one spade, he'll be reluctant to cooperate in a slam hunt.

13. May 7   Meddling Around

South dealer
Both vulnerable

       ♠ K 10 5 3
       ♡ A Q 3 2
       ◇ K 8 7 6
       ♣ 5

       ♠ 4 2
       ♡ 6 5
       ◇ A Q J 10 9 5 4
       ♣ A 7

West	North	East	South
			1◇
pass	1♡	dbl	2◇
3♣	4◇	pass	5◇
all pass			

West leads the nine of spades: ten, jack, deuce. East shifts to a low club. Plan the play.

14. May 12   Louie's Blind Spot

South dealer
Both vulnerable

       ♠ A J 8 7
       ♡ Q 4
       ◇ A 10 9
       ♣ J 10 9 5

       ♠ K Q 10 9 5 3 2
       ♡ A 5
       ◇ K J 4
       ♣ A

West	North	East	South
			1♠
pass	3♠	pass	4NT
pass	5♡	pass	6♠
all pass			

West leads the jack of hearts, and East covers dummy's queen with the king. Plan the play.

15. May 16   Behind the Back

South dealer
Both vulnerable

♠ A 4 3
♡ A 4
◇ K 10 8 7 4 3
♣ A 4

♠ K 5 2
♡ K Q 3 2
◇ A 2
♣ K Q 3 2

West	North	East	South
			1NT
pass	6NT	all pass	

West leads the jack of spades. Plan the play.

16. May 21   Cooperative Errors

South dealer
N-S vulnerable

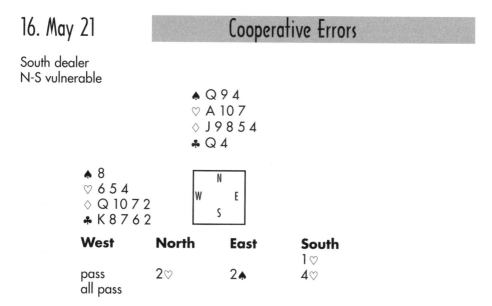

♠ Q 9 4
♡ A 10 7
◇ J 9 8 5 4
♣ Q 4

♠ 8
♡ 6 5 4
◇ Q 10 7 2
♣ K 8 7 6 2

West	North	East	South
			1♡
pass	2♡	2♠	4♡
all pass			

You lead the eight of spades. East wins with the ten and continues with the king and ace, South following. What are your discards?

13. May 7

South dealer
Both vulnerable

```
                  ♠ K 10 5 3
                  ♡ A Q 3 2
                  ◇ K 8 7 6
                  ♣ 5
   ♠ 9 8 7                        ♠ A Q J 6
   ♡ J 10 9          N            ♡ K 8 7 4
   ◇ 3          W         E       ◇ 2
   ♣ K Q J 9 4 3        S         ♣ 10 8 6 2
                  ♠ 4 2
                  ♡ 6 5
                  ◇ A Q J 10 9 5 4
                  ♣ A 7
```

West	North	East	South
			1◇
pass	1♡	dbl	2◇
3♣	4◇	pass	5◇
all pass			

Opening lead: ♠9

Cy the Cynic has defined the difference between helpful advice and out-and-out meddling: when he tells someone what they should have done, it's advice; when someone tells him, it's meddling.

In this deal, South played dummy's ten on the first spade, and East took the jack and led a club. South won, ruffed a club and drew trumps. He next led a low spade from dummy, and East rose with the queen — and endplayed himself: whether he led a club (conceding a ruff-sluff), a heart or the ace of spades, South would take the rest.

Then came the helpful advice — or the meddling, depending on where you sat. East was already annoyed with himself, and Cy, who had been West, poured fuel on the fire by telling East he should have played low on the second spade. East informed Cy he should have led the jack of hearts at Trick 1. It was quite a while until the next deal.

When South led the second spade from dummy, East knew he'd started with seven diamonds and two clubs. If South had three spades and one heart, he might have tried a heart finesse with the queen, a legitimate chance, instead of leading a second spade. Or South could run all his trumps, putting pressure on East.

In fact, South can always make five diamonds after a spade lead. After taking the ace of clubs at the second trick and ruffing a club, he runs the trumps. With three tricks to go, dummy has the king of spades and the A-Q of hearts. If East keeps the K-8 of hearts and the ace of spades, South exits with a spade to endplay East.

14. May 12

South dealer
Both vulnerable

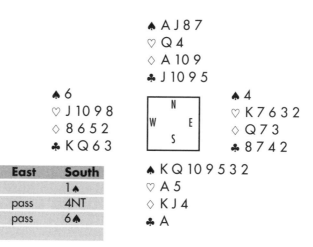

♠ A J 8 7
♡ Q 4
◇ A 10 9
♣ J 10 9 5

♠ 6
♡ J 10 9 8
◇ 8 6 5 2
♣ K Q 6 3

♠ 4
♡ K 7 6 3 2
◇ Q 7 3
♣ 8 7 4 2

♠ K Q 10 9 5 3 2
♡ A 5
◇ K J 4
♣ A

West	North	East	South
			1♠
pass	3♠	pass	4NT
pass	5♡	pass	6♠
all pass			

Opening lead: ♡J

'Do you think glasses might help me play better?' Unlucky Louie asked me in the club lounge.

'Not if you drain too many of them,' I replied.

North felt Louie needed glasses after his costly blind spot on this slam. When East covered the queen of hearts, Louie took the ace, cashed the ace of clubs, led a trump to dummy and returned the jack of clubs, pitching his last heart. West won and led another heart, and Louie ruffed, took the K-A of diamonds and led the ten of clubs for another ruffing finesse. West produced the king: down one.

'I'll have another martini,' Louie said drily. 'My chances were more than 75 percent, much better than trying to guess the queen of diamonds.'

How would you play the slam?

After South takes the ace of clubs, he can get to dummy three times with trumps to ruff dummy's remaining clubs. South then exits with a heart, and East must lead a heart, conceding a ruff-sluff, or lead a diamond, guessing the queen for declarer.

Bidding Quiz

YOU HOLD: ♠ A J 8 7 ♡ Q 4 ◇ A 10 9 ♣ J 10 9 5. Your partner opens one heart, you bid one spade and he rebids two hearts. The opponents pass. What do you say?

ANSWER: The time is right for aggression. Your tens and nines add value to your hand, especially for play in notrump, your queen of hearts will fill in partner's promised six-card suit, and you have aces on the side. Bid 3NT. If partner returns to four hearts, you won't be displeased.

15. May 16

South dealer
Both vulnerable

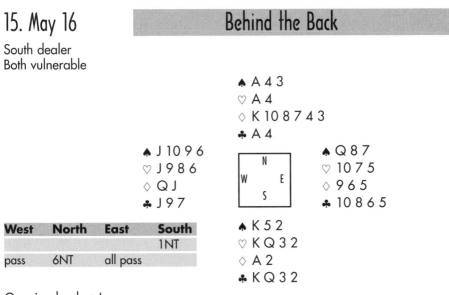

♠ A 4 3
♡ A 4
◇ K 10 8 7 4 3
♣ A 4

♠ J 10 9 6   ♠ Q 8 7
♡ J 9 8 6   ♡ 10 7 5
◇ Q J   ◇ 9 6 5
♣ J 9 7   ♣ 10 8 6 5

♠ K 5 2
♡ K Q 3 2
◇ A 2
♣ K Q 3 2

West	North	East	South
			1NT
pass	6NT	all pass	

Opening lead: ♠J

'Look at this silly play my partner perpetrated,' a player told me after a team event. 'He won the first spade in dummy, pondered — and let the ten of diamonds ride! West won and led another spade, and partner won and took the ace of diamonds. Luckily, his play cost only an overtrick. The other South in 6NT took thirteen tricks, of course.'

I always hate to hear someone backstab a partner — especially with misguided comments. To make 6NT, South must play the diamonds for one loser. If they break 3-2, any play works. If East has, say, Q-9-6-5, or if West has Q-J-9-6, South is sunk; he can handle a 4-1 break only if East has a singleton honor or if either defender has the singleton nine.

If West has the bare nine, East can't gain by covering the ten: South loses only one diamond. If East covered the ten with an honor or played the nine, South would take the ace, return a diamond and cover West's card.

What North should have done behind South's back was pat it.

16. May 21

South dealer
N-S vulnerable

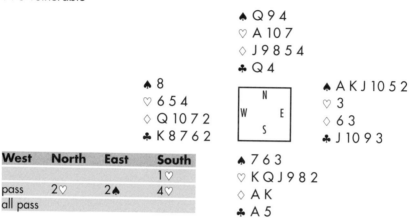

♠ Q 9 4
♡ A 10 7
◇ J 9 8 5 4
♣ Q 4

♠ 8
♡ 6 5 4
◇ Q 10 7 2
♣ K 8 7 6 2

♠ A K J 10 5 2
♡ 3
◇ 6 3
♣ J 10 9 3

♠ 7 6 3
♡ K Q J 9 8 2
◇ A K
♣ A 5

West	North	East	South
			1♡
pass	2♡	2♠	4♡
all pass			

Opening lead: ♠8

'I know God took only six days to create the world,' a disgruntled player at the club told me, 'but that was because He was working alone. If He'd had a partner to contend with, the job wouldn't have been finished on schedule — or done right.'

That impious remark was prompted by this deal: East-West could have beaten four hearts but didn't — and neither player was happy with his partner.

When West led a spade, East took the ten, king and ace, and West discarded the eight and then the deuce of clubs. East then led a club.

'I thought my partner had the ace of clubs,' East contended. 'But South produced the ace, cashed the A-K of diamonds, led a trump to the seven, ruffed a diamond, led a trump to the ten and ruffed a diamond. He drew trumps with the ace, threw his last club on the good jack of diamonds and took the thirteenth trick with a trump.'

Do you see how East-West could beat four hearts? Which defender was responsible for letting South get home?

After the defense wins the first three tricks, someone must lead a trump. This play removes a vital entry to dummy before South has started the diamonds, and South must lose a club.

East can infer that West doesn't have the ace of clubs; otherwise West would ruff East's winning spade at the third trick and cash the setting trick. But only West knows he has three low trumps (he might have Q-x-x) and the diamonds well stopped. Therefore, West should ruff East's winner at Trick 3 and lead a trump to defeat the contract.

17. May 24 — Louie's Lot in Life

South dealer
N-S vulnerable

```
            ♠ Q J 10 8
            ♡ A 4
            ◇ A Q J
            ♣ J 9 8 2

            ♠ A K 9 7 6 4 3 2
            ♡ J 5
            ◇ 9 6
            ♣ A
```

West	North	East	South
			1♠
pass	3♠	pass	4♣
pass	4◇	pass	5♣
pass	6♠	all pass	

West leads the ten of hearts. Plan the play.

18. May 27 — Before You Abuse

North dealer
Both vulnerable

```
            ♠ Q J 3
            ♡ A K 8
            ◇ 8 5 3
            ♣ A 8 6 4

            ♠ 10 9 8 7 4
            ♡ Q J 4
            ◇ A J
            ♣ K Q 3
```

West	North	East	South
	1♣	pass	1♠
pass	2♠	pass	4♠
all pass			

West leads the ten of clubs. You win with the queen and lead a trump, and West takes the king and leads the nine of clubs. You take the king and lead another trump, and West produces the ace and persists with the seven of clubs. What do you play from dummy?

19. May 30 — Louie's Tall Tale

South dealer
N-S vulnerable

```
                    ♠ J 10 6
                    ♡ 6 5 3 2
                    ◇ K J 9 6
                    ♣ K 2

                    ♠ A K Q
                    ♡ A Q 10
                    ◇ A Q
                    ♣ A Q 6 5 3
```

West	North	East	South
			3NT
pass	6NT	all pass	

West leads the nine of spades. Plan the play.

20. June 3 — His Own Fault

South dealer
Both vulnerable

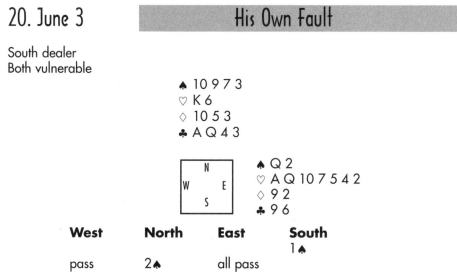

```
          ♠ 10 9 7 3
          ♡ K 6
          ◇ 10 5 3
          ♣ A Q 4 3

    ┌─────────┐        ♠ Q 2
    │    N    │        ♡ A Q 10 7 5 4 2
    │ W     E │        ◇ 9 2
    │    S    │        ♣ 9 6
    └─────────┘
```

West	North	East	South
			1♠
pass	2♠	all pass	

West leads the ace of diamonds, suggesting he has the king also. Plan the defense.

Louie's Lot in Life

South dealer
N-S vulnerable

```
                  ♠ Q J 10 8
                  ♡ A 4
                  ◇ A Q J
                  ♣ J 9 8 2
    ♠ 5                            ♠ —
    ♡ Q 10 9          N            ♡ K 8 7 6 3 2
    ◇ 7 4 2       W       E        ◇ K 10 8 5 3
    ♣ K 7 6 5 4 3     S            ♣ Q 10
                  ♠ A K 9 7 6 4 3 2
                  ♡ J 5
                  ◇ 9 6
                  ♣ A
```

West	North	East	South
			1♠
pass	3♠	pass	4♣
pass	4◇	pass	5♣
pass	6♠	all pass	

Opening lead: ♡10

'It's my lot in life,' Unlucky Louie told me, 'to receive the killing opening lead against every slam I bid.'

In this deal, West unerringly led a heart against Louie's contract of six spades. Louie took the ace, led a trump to his hand and returned a diamond to finesse the jack. East produced the king and cashed the king of hearts.

'With no heart lead, not even I would go down,' Louie grumbled.

Some people build a skyscraper on their lot in life, others park cars. Louie's lot seems to be vacant; if he tried all his chances, he'd make the slam even against a heart lead.

Louie should lead a club to his ace at Trick 2. When East's ten falls, Louie returns a trump to dummy and ruffs a club, dropping the queen. He gets back with a trump and leads the nine of clubs, pitching his last heart when East shows out.

West takes the king of clubs and leads a diamond, but Louie steps up with the ace and throws his last diamond on the good jack of clubs.

Bidding Quiz

YOU HOLD: ♠ 5 ♡ Q 10 9 ◇ 7 4 2 ♣ K 7 6 5 4 3. Your partner opens one club, and the next player doubles. What do you say?

ANSWER: You should preempt as high as the vulnerability allows. If not vulnerable, jump to four clubs; if vulnerable, try three clubs. With a strong hand, you'd redouble; but an immediate jump promises a weak, distributional hand with great support. If the opponents bid four spades, your partner can judge whether to sacrifice.

18. May 27

North dealer
Both vulnerable

♠ Q J 3
♡ A K 8
◇ 8 5 3
♣ A 8 6 4

♠ A K
♡ 9 7 6 3
◇ K 10 6
♣ J 10 9 7

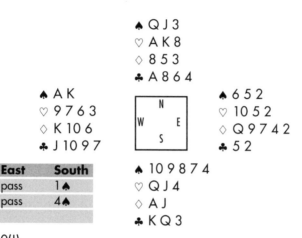

♠ 6 5 2
♡ 10 5 2
◇ Q 9 7 4 2
♣ 5 2

♠ 10 9 8 7 4
♡ Q J 4
◇ A J
♣ K Q 3

West	North	East	South
	1♣	pass	1♠
pass	2♠	pass	4♠
all pass			

Opening lead: ♣10(!)

Cy the Cynic was suffering through a losing streak — and had begun to take it out on his partners.

'Before you berate your partner,' I admonished Cy, 'you ought to walk a mile in his shoes.'

'That's a good idea,' the Cynic growled. 'Then I can berate him, and I'll have a pair of shoes and a one-mile head start.'

I threw up my hands; but that day, Cy cut into a Chicago game and wound up facing Grapefruit, our member whose disposition is acid-tipped whether he's winning or losing. Cy was South, and West found a tricky opening lead: the ten of clubs. Cy won with the king and led a trump, and West won and continued with the nine of clubs. Cy took the queen and led another trump to West's ace.

West then led the seven of clubs. Cy put up dummy's ace, expecting to claim an over-trick when East's jack fell — and was stunned when East ruffed. East then led a diamond, and Cy had to lose a diamond.

Grapefruit wasn't stunned; he was mad. 'If your brains were dynamite,' he told Cy, 'you couldn't blow your nose.' And Grapefruit launched into a critique of Cy's ancestry, while Cy cowered in his chair.

On the third club, Cy must play the eight. If East produced the jack, Cy would win the diamond return, draw trumps and go to dummy to throw the jack of diamonds on the ace of clubs. His actual play might have gained an overtrick but risked the contract.

Cy's losing streak is still on, but he's treating partners with more compassion.

19. May 30

South dealer
N-S vulnerable

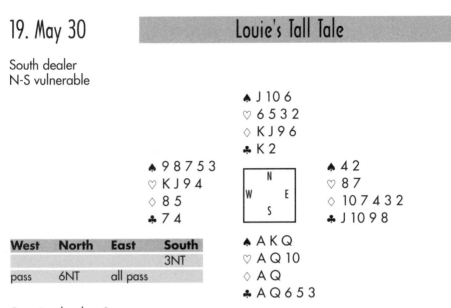

```
                    ♠ J 10 6
                    ♡ 6 5 3 2
                    ◇ K J 9 6
                    ♣ K 2
    ♠ 9 8 7 5 3              ♠ 4 2
    ♡ K J 9 4        N       ♡ 8 7
    ◇ 8 5        W       E   ◇ 10 7 4 3 2
    ♣ 7 4            S       ♣ J 10 9 8
                    ♠ A K Q
                    ♡ A Q 10
                    ◇ A Q
                    ♣ A Q 6 5 3
```

West	North	East	South
			3NT
pass	6NT	all pass	

Opening lead: ♠9

I'd read about a medical theory that people are slightly taller in the morning. When I mentioned it to Unlucky Louie, he sighed.

'All I know is, I'm always short at the end of the month,' he said, 'and right now I'm so broke I can't even pay attention.'

Louie's attention span was lacking in this deal. He took the ace of spades and the A-Q of diamonds, led a club to the king and cashed the K-J of diamonds, pitching the Q-10 of hearts. Louie next took the A-Q of clubs. When West showed out, Louie had to concede a club to East, who promptly cashed his fifth diamond!

Decide how you'd play the slam.

Louie was unlucky (as usual) to find East with five diamonds as well as four clubs, but Louie can leave little to luck by playing low from dummy on the first club.

East wins and returns a heart, and Louie takes the ace, goes to the king of clubs and throws hearts on the K-J of diamonds. He can then return to his hand and run the clubs and spades for twelve tricks.

Bidding Quiz

YOU HOLD: ♠ J 10 6 ♡ 6 5 3 2 ◇ K J 9 6 ♣ K 2. Dealer, on your left, opens one heart. Your partner doubles, you respond two diamonds and partner then bids two spades. The opponents pass. What do you say?

ANSWER: If your partner held an average hand, he'd have overcalled one spade. By doubling before bidding a suit, he promises great extra strength. If your hand were any stronger, you'd have jumped at your first turn; hence bid four spades now.

20. June 3

His Own Fault

South dealer
Both vulnerable

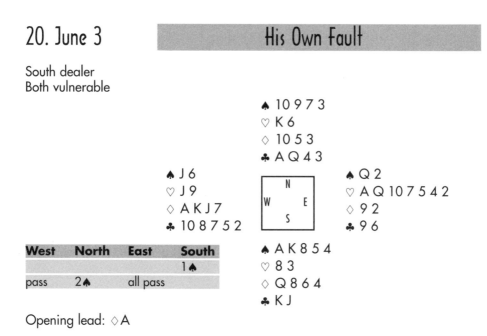

```
                    ♠ 10 9 7 3
                    ♡ K 6
                    ◊ 10 5 3
                    ♣ A Q 4 3
    ♠ J 6                          ♠ Q 2
    ♡ J 9            N             ♡ A Q 10 7 5 4 2
    ◊ A K J 7     W     E          ◊ 9 2
    ♣ 10 8 7 5 2      S            ♣ 9 6
                    ♠ A K 8 5 4
                    ♡ 8 3
                    ◊ Q 8 6 4
                    ♣ K J
```

West	North	East	South
			1♠
pass	2♠	all pass	

Opening lead: ◊A

A player at the club confided that he'd gotten himself in the doghouse.

'I know any man who wins an argument with his wife has only himself to blame,' he said, 'but after we misdefended this deal, I couldn't help defending myself.'

My friend said his wife, sitting West, led the ace of diamonds, and he played the nine with his 9-2 doubleton. She continued with the king and a low diamond, and he ruffed.

'I led a trump next,' my friend said, 'hoping I'd get the A-Q of hearts later. South drew trumps, took the K-J of clubs, led a trump to dummy, threw his hearts on the A-Q of clubs and made an overtrick.

'When my wife saw my hand, her reaction was one long groan cut up into words. First she asked me why I hadn't bid hearts; then she wanted to know why I'd played the nine of diamonds. One word led to another, and we played the rest of the deals — and went to bed last night — in silence.'

'I wouldn't have bid three hearts either,' I said, 'but she was right about the defense. On the first diamond, you should signal "attitude" — whether you like diamonds — not "count". Since you want a heart shift, not a diamond continuation, you must play the deuce.'

If West shifts to a heart at Trick 2 — the logical shift — East takes the A-Q and leads a diamond back. West scores the jack and king and leads a fourth diamond, and East over-ruffs dummy with the queen and leads a third heart. South can't stop West from winning a trump trick with the jack, and East-West collect 200 points and go to bed happy.

21. June 8 — Silly Game

South dealer
Both vulnerable

```
              ♠ 8 6 3
              ♡ A 7 3
              ◇ 9 7 4
              ♣ A Q 7 2

              ♠ A 7 4
              ♡ K J 4
              ◇ A Q 8 2
              ♣ K J 5
```

West	North	East	South
			1NT
pass	3NT	all pass	

West leads the queen of spades, and East overtakes with the king. Plan the play.

22. June 12 — Mortality Conference

South dealer
Both vulnerable

```
              ♠ K 10 5 4
              ♡ A 5 4
              ◇ 7 3
              ♣ 10 9 7 3

              ♠ A Q 7
              ♡ K 8
              ◇ A Q J 10 9
              ♣ Q 8 4
```

West	North	East	South
			1◇
pass	1♠	pass	2NT
pass	3NT	all pass	

West leads the three of hearts. Plan the play.

23. June 15

Slim Margin

North dealer
Both vulnerable

♠ K 6 2
♡ A 7 5 3
♢ A Q J 10 3
♣ 3

♠ A Q 7 4
♡ K 8
♢ K 9
♣ A J 7 6 2

West	North	East	South
	1♢	pass	2♣
pass	2♢	pass	2♠
pass	2NT	pass	3♢
pass	3♠	pass	6♠
all pass			

West leads the king of clubs. Plan the play.

24. June 16

Contract in Stitches

North dealer
N-S vulnerable

♠ A Q 9 7
♡ J
♢ Q J 8 5
♣ A K 7 3

♠ K J 10
♡ K 8 7 3
♢ K 10 9
♣ Q 4 2

West	North	East	South
	1♢	1♡	2NT
pass	3NT	all pass	

West leads the five of hearts. East takes the ace and returns the queen. Plan the play.

21. June 8

South dealer
Both vulnerable

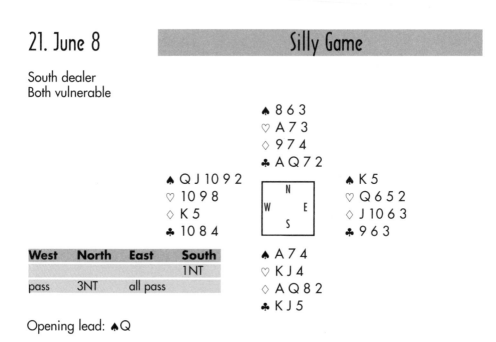

West	**North**	**East**	**South**
			1NT
pass	3NT	all pass	

Opening lead: ♠Q

'My husband says bridge is a silly, childish game,' a player at the club remarked to me.

'That's probably because he thinks his wife can beat him at it,' I observed.

'When he was declarer in this deal,' she went on, 'East overtook the queen of spades with the king. My dear love played low, won the next spade, ran four clubs and led a diamond to finesse with the queen.

'That lost, West ran the spades and my husband left to watch a basketball game on TV. He said bridge is just a guessing game; if he finessed in hearts instead of in diamonds, he'd make the contract. Is there any hope for him?'

I told my friend to show her husband — gently — how 3NT was cold, hoping to rekindle his interest. After South takes the second spade, he cashes three clubs (not four) and then leads dummy's last spade.

West can take three spades but must then lead a heart or a diamond. South gets a free finesse and his ninth trick no matter where the red-suit honors lie.

Bidding Quiz

YOU HOLD: ♠ 8 6 3 ♡ A 7 3 ◇ 9 7 4 ♣ A Q 7 2. Your partner opens one spade, you respond two clubs, he next bids two diamonds and you return to two spades. Partner then bids three spades. The opponents pass. What do you say?

ANSWER: Your first two bids promised about 10 points, a club suit and some spade support. Partner is still interested in game, but since you have minimum values and no helping honors in either of his suits, pass.

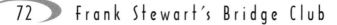

22. June 12

South dealer
Both vulnerable

```
                      ♠ K 10 5 4
                      ♡ A 5 4
                      ◇ 7 3
                      ♣ 10 9 7 3
        ♠ 8 3                          ♠ J 9 6 2
        ♡ J 9 6 3 2          N         ♡ Q 10 7
        ◇ 8 4           W        E      ◇ K 6 5 2
        ♣ A K J 2            S          ♣ 6 5
                      ♠ A Q 7
                      ♡ K 8
                      ◇ A Q J 10 9
                      ♣ Q 8 4
```

West	North	East	South
			1◇
pass	1♠	pass	2NT
pass	3NT	all pass	

Opening lead: ♡3

'My husband's a hypochondriac,' a friend complained to me. 'He wouldn't visit the Dead Sea without asking what it died of. And yes, the best part of his bridge is the post-mortem.

'He took the ace of hearts and led a diamond, finessing the ten. He next cashed the ace, queen and king of spades, hoping the jack would fall and give him four spade tricks. When West discarded, my husband led another diamond to the jack and then laid down the ace.

'West discarded again, and East won the next diamond. He took the jack of spades and led a club, and West took three clubs. Down one.

'In the inevitable post-mortem, my hubby ascribed it all to bad luck, but I say the contract's demise was preventable.'

It was a common cause of death: the failure to count tricks. South has two heart tricks and at least four diamonds; hence he needs only three spades. After winning the first diamond finesse, South should lead a spade to the king and finesse again in diamonds to assure the contract.

Bidding Quiz

YOU HOLD: ♠ 8 3 ♡ J 9 6 3 2 ◇ 8 4 ♣ A K J 2. Dealer, on your left, opens one club. Your partner doubles, and the next player passes. What do you say?

ANSWER: Bid two hearts, promising about 10 points. You may be tempted to pass for a penalty, but you won't hurt your opponent badly in one club doubled and may be cold for game in hearts. To pass, you'd need long, solid clubs and no interest in a contract of your own.

Slim Margin

North dealer
Both vulnerable

```
              ♠ K 6 2
              ♡ A 7 5 3
              ◇ A Q J 10 3
              ♣ 3
  ♠ J 10 8 3              ♠ 9 5
  ♡ Q 6          N        ♡ J 10 9 4 2
  ◇ 7 2      W     E      ◇ 8 6 5 4
  ♣ K Q 10 9 8    S       ♣ 5 4
              ♠ A Q 7 4
              ♡ K 8
              ◇ K 9
              ♣ A J 7 6 2
```

West	North	East	South
	1◇	pass	2♣
pass	2◇	pass	2♠
pass	2NT	pass	3◇
pass	3♠	pass	6♠
all pass			

Opening lead: ♣K

Grapefruit, our club member with the acid disposition, had to go in for gall bladder surgery. He got a get-well card from the club: 'The Board of Directors has voted seven to six to wish you a speedy recovery.'

A seven-to-six margin in trumps is playable but often precarious. In this deal declarer took the ace of clubs, ruffed a club, returned a heart to his hand and ruffed a club. East overruffed, and South also lost a trump and a club to West.

Six diamonds on the 5-2 fit would be easier, but South makes six spades on the 4-3 fit if he keeps control of trumps to run the diamonds. Since the missing trumps are likely to break 4-2, South must lead a trump at Trick 2 and play low from dummy.

If East shifts to a heart, South takes the king, ruffs a club, cashes the king of trumps, returns to the king of diamonds and draws trumps with the A-Q.

South can then run the diamonds. He wins three trumps in his hand, two hearts, a club, a club ruff and five diamonds.

Bidding Quiz

YOU HOLD: ♠ J 10 8 3 ♡ Q 6 ◇ 7 2 ♣ K Q 10 9 8. Your partner opens one heart, you respond one spade and he then bids two diamonds. The opponents pass. What do you say?

ANSWER: You couldn't respond two clubs — your hand was too weak — and you must not bid 2NT now since you'd promise about 11 points. Since partner has at least five hearts, bid two hearts, promising heart tolerance but at most 9 points.

24. June 16

Contract in Stitches

North dealer
N-S vulnerable

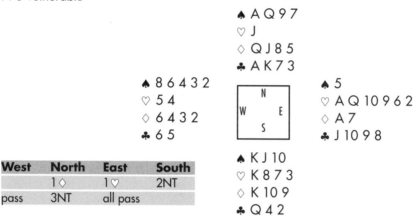

♠ A Q 9 7
♡ J
◇ Q J 8 5
♣ A K 7 3

♠ 8 6 4 3 2
♡ 5 4
◇ 6 4 3 2
♣ 6 5

♠ 5
♡ A Q 10 9 6 2
◇ A 7
♣ J 10 9 8

♠ K J 10
♡ K 8 7 3
◇ K 10 9
♣ Q 4 2

West	North	East	South
	1◇	1♡	2NT
pass	3NT	all pass	

Opening lead: ♡ 5

Grapefruit, our sourpuss member, returned to the club in style after his gall bladder surgery. After snarling that the hospital needed a recovery room next to the cashier's office, Grapefruit announced that he would recover the cost of his stay in the afternoon's penny Chicago game.

As North, Grapefruit was willing to raise South's 2NT to game. When West led a heart, East took the ace and returned the queen, winning. South won the third heart and led a diamond, and East happily won and ran the hearts. Down two.

I could see Grapefruit was near a relapse. If South starts instead by taking four spade tricks, East is stuck. East can pitch a diamond and one heart, but if he throws a club next, South wins four club tricks; and if East throws a second heart, South forces out the ace of diamonds safely.

'Sorry,' South said. 'Hope you won't hold a grudge.'

'I don't hold grudges,' growled Grapefruit, 'not even against people who've done things I'll never forgive.'

Bidding Quiz

YOU HOLD: ♠ A Q 9 7 ♡ J ◇ Q J 8 5 ♣ A K 7 3. Dealer, on your right, opens three hearts. You double, and your partner bids three spades. The opponents pass. What do you say?

ANSWER: Your double forced partner to bid at the three- or four-level. (He could pass, but only with strength in hearts.) Since you promised at least 17 points, and since partner may have a terrible hand with weak spades, pass. He'd have bid four spades himself with a fair hand.

PART 3

Summer

1. June 18   Three Opponents

South dealer
E-W vulnerable

```
          ♠ A K 4
          ♡ 9 5
          ◇ K Q 10 9 4
          ♣ J 7 3
♠ 8 3 2
♡ 8 7 3 2        N
◇ A 7 6 3    W       E
♣ K Q           S
```

West	North	East	South
			1♠
pass	2◇	pass	2♡
pass	3♠	pass	4♠
all pass			

You lead the king of clubs: three, ten, deuce. Plan the defense.

2. June 20   Deepest Finesse

North dealer
Both vulnerable

```
          ♠ A 5 4
          ♡ K 5 4 2
          ◇ K 7 5
          ♣ A Q 7


          ♠ Q 9 8 7 6 2
          ♡ 6 3
          ◇ A 6
          ♣ K 9 5
```

West	North	East	South
	1NT	pass	4♠
all pass			

West leads the jack of diamonds. Plan the play.

3. June 24

North dealer
Neither vulnerable

        ♠ A K 10 5
        ♡ 10 3
        ◊ 7 6 2
        ♣ A K Q J

        ♠ Q J 2
        ♡ A Q J 9 8 2
        ◊ J 8 3
        ♣ 5

West	North	East	South
	1♣	pass	1♡
pass	1♠	pass	3♡
pass	4♡	all pass	

West leads the king of diamonds and continues with the queen and ace, East following.
West shifts to a spade, and you win in dummy and let the ten of trumps ride, winning. On
a second trump to your jack, West discards. How do you continue?

4. June 27

South dealer
E-W vulnerable

        ♠ 9 4 3
        ♡ K Q 8 6 4
        ◊ 9 4
        ♣ A K 3

        ♠ A K J 10 8 2
        ♡ 2
        ◊ K Q 6 5
        ♣ 7 4

West	North	East	South
			1♠
pass	2♡	pass	2♠
pass	4♠	all pass	

West leads the queen of clubs. Plan the play.

South dealer
E-W vulnerable

```
              ♠ A K 4
              ♡ 9 5
              ◇ K Q 10 9 4
              ♣ J 7 3
♠ 8 3 2                      ♠ J 7
♡ 8 7 3 2        N           ♡ 10 6 4
◇ A 7 6 3    W       E       ◇ J 5 2
♣ K Q           S           ♣ A 10 9 8 4
              ♠ Q 10 9 6 5
              ♡ A K Q J
              ◇ 8
              ♣ 6 5 2
```

West	North	East	South
			1♠
pass	2◇	pass	2♡
pass	3♠	pass	4♠
all pass			

Opening lead: ♣K

'I heard somewhere that it's a partnership game,' Cy the Cynic sighed, 'but sometimes I feel like I have three opponents, not two.'

'I know what you mean,' I said.

Cy produced this deal. 'I was East,' he said, 'and my partner led the king of clubs and then the queen. I considered overtaking with the ace, but what if he'd had another club?'

'When I played low, partner gave me a sour look and led a trump. Declarer won and led a diamond. Partner took the ace and led another trump, and then declarer threw his last club on a high diamond and made the contract.

'Partner claims I should have worked it out. He said with K-Q-x of clubs, he'd lead low at the second trick.'

'Maybe,' I remarked, 'but he put you to a needless guess. He must cash the ace of diamonds at Trick 2. When he leads the queen of clubs next, you have nothing to lose by overtaking to return a club.'

Always try to make things easy for your partner. Three-to-one odds are tough to overcome.

Bidding Quiz

YOU HOLD: ♠ A K 4 ♡ 9 5 ◇ K Q 10 9 4 ♣ J 7 3. Your partner opens one club, you respond one diamond and he bids one heart. The opponents pass. What do you say?

ANSWER: Bid 3NT. After opener has bid twice, it's up to responder to place the contract or suggest a contract. Since you have a hand worth an opening bid, balanced distribution and spade strength, you know where to play. You'd bid 2NT if your king of spades were the jack.

2. June 20

North dealer
Both vulnerable

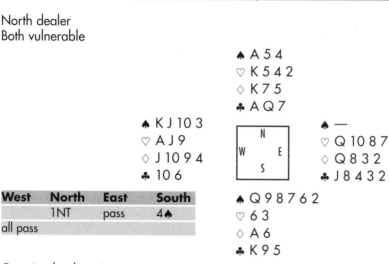

♠ A 5 4
♡ K 5 4 2
◇ K 7 5
♣ A Q 7

♠ K J 10 3
♡ A J 9
◇ J 10 9 4
♣ 10 6

♠ —
♡ Q 10 8 7
◇ Q 8 3 2
♣ J 8 4 3 2

♠ Q 9 8 7 6 2
♡ 6 3
◇ A 6
♣ K 9 5

West	North	East	South
	1NT	pass	4♠
all pass			

Opening lead: ◇ J

'Yesterday I tied an unbreakable record,' Unlucky Louie said proudly. 'What's the deepest finesse possible?'

'Assuming you lead a deuce to finesse against a three,' I replied, 'you could win with a four.'

Louie told me he won the first diamond with the ace and saw he might lose two hearts and two, or even three, trumps; but if the ace of hearts was onside, he could afford a safety play to guard against three trump losers.

'At the second trick I led a heart to the king as a discovery play,' Louie said. 'If East had the ace, I'd have hoped for a 2-2 trump break, but when the king won, I returned a club to my hand and led a trump. When West followed with the three, I put in dummy's four.'

'Well done,' I said.

'When you get as many horrible breaks as I do,' Louie shrugged, 'you better know how to handle them.'

If East can beat dummy's four of trumps, Louie cashes the ace later, losing at most one more trump. When East actually discarded on the first trump, Louie cashed the ace and conceded two trumps and a heart.

Bidding Quiz

YOU HOLD: ♠ Q 9 8 7 6 2 ♡ 6 3 ◇ A 6 ♣ K 9 5. Your partner opens one heart, you bid one spade and he rebids two hearts. The opponents pass. What do you say?

ANSWER: Partner promises a minimum opening bid with a six-card heart suit; he'd try hard to avoid rebidding a five-card suit. Since your game chances are nil, pass. To rebid two spades would accomplish nothing and might land you in a 6-0 fit instead of the known 6-2 fit.

Book Learning

North dealer
Neither vulnerable

```
              ♠ A K 10 5
              ♡ 10 3
              ◇ 7 6 2
              ♣ A K Q J
  ♠ 9 6 3                    ♠ 8 7 4
  ♡ 4            N            ♡ K 7 6 5
  ◇ A K Q 4   W     E         ◇ 10 9 5
  ♣ 9 7 4 3 2     S           ♣ 10 8 6
              ♠ Q J 2
              ♡ A Q J 9 8 2
              ◇ J 8 3
              ♣ 5
```

West	North	East	South
	1♣	pass	1♡
Pass	1♠	pass	3♡
Pass	4♡	all pass	

Opening lead: ◇K

'Read any good books lately?' I asked at the club.

'I just finished one about levitation,' Cy the Cynic replied. 'Couldn't put it down.'

'Somebody gave me a book on milk production,' Unlucky Louie offered, 'but I just skimmed it.'

'I knew I wouldn't get a straight answer from you clowns,' I groaned. 'I mean bridge books. This deal could be straight from a chapter on play techniques.'

West cashes three diamonds and leads a spade. South wins with the ten, lets the ten of trumps ride and leads a trump to the jack. West shows out, and South seems doomed to lose a trump.

South leads a club to dummy, ruffs a club, leads a spade to dummy and ruffs a club. He gets back with a spade and leads a club at the twelfth trick, trapping East's king of trumps.

'It's a Double Grand Coup,' I said. 'Declarer ruffs two winners to reach the coup position.'

'Very nice,' Louie said, 'but I'm starting a book on trees.'

'You'll probably just leaf through it,' I observed.

Bidding Quiz

YOU HOLD: ♠ A K 10 5 ♡ 10 3 ◇ 7 6 2 ♣ A K Q J. Dealer, on your right, opens one diamond. What do you say?

ANSWER: A miserable problem. Since you have no strength in diamonds but may have a game if your partner holds a few points, to 'trap pass' isn't attractive. But you can't double without heart support or overcall 1NT without a diamond trick. Bid one spade and hope partner doesn't notice you have only a four-card suit.

4. June 27

South dealer
E-W vulnerable

```
                          ♠ 9 4 3
                          ♡ K Q 8 6 4
                          ◇ 9 4
                          ♣ A K 3
         ♠ —                              ♠ Q 7 6 5
         ♡ J 9 5 3          N             ♡ A 10 7
         ◇ A J 10 8 3   W       E         ◇ 7 2
         ♣ Q J 10 5          S            ♣ 9 8 6 2
                          ♠ A K J 10 8 2
                          ♡ 2
                          ◇ K Q 6 5
                          ♣ 7 4
```

West	North	East	South
			1♠
pass	2♡	pass	2♠
pass	4♠	all pass	

Opening lead: ♣Q

An old man entered my club, looking as if he'd come to town on a watermelon truck, and sat down to watch. He wore overalls and dangled a corncob pipe.

South took the ace of clubs and played a diamond to his king and West's ace. The old man squirmed but said nothing. South won the club return, lost the king of hearts to East's ace, ruffed the next club and led the jack of trumps! He was safe if East took the queen, but East played low.

When South took the queen of diamonds and ruffed a diamond next, East overruffed and led the queen of trumps. South lost a diamond and went down, and the oldster shook his head.

'How do you play it, Grandpa?' South sneered.

The reply came in a drawl you could pour over pancakes: 'If you got to swaller a frog, do it quick. Lead the king of hearts at Trick 2, win the club return, shed a diamond on the queen of hearts and lead a diamond. You ruff a diamond with the nine of trumps later, and you're home free.'

You know what? He was right.

Bidding Quiz

YOU HOLD: ♠ — ♡ J 9 5 3 ◇ A J 10 8 3 ♣ Q J 10 5. Your partner opens one spade, you bid 1NT and he rebids two spades. The opponents pass. What do you say?

ANSWER: Pass. You responded conservatively with 1NT because you feared a misfit, and things have grown worse. Partner has minimum values with at least six spades. He may manage eight tricks in spades, but if you bid again, you risk a large minus if the opponents start to double.

5. June 30   Father of the Bride

North dealer
N-S vulnerable

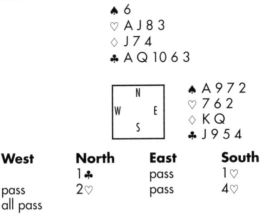

```
                    ♠ 6
                    ♡ A J 8 3
                    ◇ J 7 4
                    ♣ A Q 10 6 3
                                        ♠ A 9 7 2
              ┌─────────────┐          ♡ 7 6 2
              │      N      │          ◇ K Q
              │  W       E  │          ♣ J 9 5 4
              │      S      │
              └─────────────┘
```

West	North	East	South
	1♣	pass	1♡
pass	2♡	pass	4♡
all pass			

West leads the queen of spades. Plan the defense.

6. July 1   Cool, Calm, Collected

South dealer
Both vulnerable

```
                    ♠ Q J 9 2
                    ♡ A K J 9
                    ◇ 10 6 2
                    ♣ Q 5

                    ♠ A K 10 3
                    ♡ 6
                    ◇ A K J 9 4
                    ♣ A 6 2
```

West	North	East	South
			1◇
pass	1♡	pass	2♠
pass	5♠	pass	6♣
pass	6♠	all pass	

West leads the jack of clubs. Plan the play.

7. July 3   Good Luck and Bad

North dealer
E-W vulnerable

```
              ♠ A 9 4 3
              ♡ K 5
              ◇ J 4 3 2
              ♣ A J 6

              ♠ K Q J 5 2
              ♡ J 9 6 3
              ◇ 7 6
              ♣ Q 8
```

West	North	East	South
	1◇	pass	1♠
pass	2♠	pass	4♠(!)
all pass			

West leads the seven of hearts. You play low from dummy, and East takes the ace and shifts to the queen of diamonds and another diamond. West wins with the king and exits with the deuce of hearts to dummy's king.

You lead a trump to your king and return the queen of clubs: king, ace. When you lead a trump to your queen, West discards. What now?

8. July 7   Late-Night Consult

South dealer
N-S vulnerable

```
              ♠ A 5 3 2
              ♡ 10 3
              ◇ 7 4 2
              ♣ A J 10 8

              ♠ K Q J
              ♡ A K 8 7 4
              ◇ A K Q J
              ♣ K
```

West	North	East	South
			2♣
pass	3♣	pass	3♡
pass	3♠	pass	6NT
all pass			

West leads the ten of diamonds. Plan the play. (Assume no suit breaks well.)

5. June 30

North dealer
N-S vulnerable

```
                          ♠ 6
                          ♡ A J 8 3
                          ◇ J 7 4
                          ♣ A Q 10 6 3
        ♠ Q J 10 8 3                        ♠ A 9 7 2
        ♡ 9               ┌─────────┐       ♡ 7 6 2
        ◇ A 10 6 2        │    N    │       ◇ K Q
        ♣ 8 7 2          W│         │E      ♣ J 9 5 4
                          │    S    │
                          └─────────┘
                          ♠ K 5 4
```

West	North	East	South
	1♣	pass	1♡
pass	2♡	pass	4♡
all pass			

♡ K Q 10 5 4
◇ 9 8 5 3
♣ K

Opening lead: ♠Q

Unlucky Louie's oldest girl had gotten married over the weekend, and he looked a little frazzled.

'A man spends his life keeping the wolf from the door,' Louie sighed, 'and then his daughter brings one home.'

Louie mismanaged a marriage of his own as East. He took the ace of spades and led the king and then the queen of diamonds. West signaled high for a continuation, but Louie couldn't oblige. When he led a trump next, South drew trumps and took the rest, throwing his last two diamonds on dummy's high clubs.

To defeat the contract, Louie must lead the queen of diamonds first and then the king. This abnormal play should wake up West: he'll overtake and lead a third diamond, letting Louie ruff for the setting trick.

'So did the wedding go off without a hitch — or was it a big success?' I asked.

'I was really proud of my little girl,' Louie told me. 'When the minister asked if she took the groom for richer or poorer, she said, "For richer".'

Bidding Quiz

YOU HOLD: ♠ Q J 10 8 3 ♡ 9 ◇ A 10 6 2 ♣ 8 7 2. Your partner opens 1NT, and the next player passes. What do you say?

ANSWER: This hand is too strong to sign off in two spades but too weak to force to game. To invite, start by bidding two clubs, Stayman. If partner next bids two spades, your hand improves and you'll bid four spades. If he bids two diamonds, denying a four-card major suit, or two hearts, then you'll just bid two spades.

6. July 1

South dealer
Both vulnerable

```
              ♠ Q J 9 2
              ♡ A K J 9
              ◇ 10 6 2
              ♣ Q 5
♠ 8 5                        ♠ 7 6 4
♡ 10 7 4 2      N           ♡ Q 8 5 3
◇ Q 5       W       E       ◇ 8 7 3
♣ J 10 9 8 4     S          ♣ K 7 3
              ♠ A K 10 3
              ♡ 6
              ◇ A K J 9 4
              ♣ A 6 2
```

West	North	East	South
			1◇
pass	1♡	pass	2♠
pass	5♠	pass	6♣
pass	6♠	all pass	

Opening lead: ♣J

My friend the English professor grumbles that students come to him ill-prepared. He told me he asked a class for an example of a collective noun (such as 'orchestra'), and the responses he got were 'wastebasket,' 'flypaper' and 'vacuum cleaner.'

The prof also thinks his partners are collectively hopeless at dummy play. In this deal, with the prof watching as North, West's jack of clubs collected the queen, king and ace, and after South collected his thoughts, he took the ace of trumps and the ace of diamonds and drew the remaining trumps.

South next let the ten of diamonds ride, but West won and cashed the ten of clubs. Down one.

I can't say the prof was cool, calm and collected. 'Sheer butchery,' he sighed. 'After you win the first club, draw trumps and cash the top diamonds. When the queen falls, you're home. This play gives you two chances: if the queen of diamonds doesn't fall, you try a heart finesse with the jack to discard your losing clubs.'

Bidding Quiz

YOU HOLD: ♠ Q J 9 2 ♡ A K J 9 ◇ 10 6 2 ♣ Q 5. Your partner opens one club, you respond one heart and he next bids one spade. The opponents pass. What do you say?

ANSWER: Now that partner has bid twice, you must place the contract or suggest a contract. Since you have a fit in spades and enough strength for game even if he has minimum values, bid four spades. You'd bid three spades, invitational, if your king of hearts were a low heart.

7. July 3

North dealer
E-W vulnerable

Good Luck and Bad

```
                     ♠ A 9 4 3
                     ♡ K 5
                     ◇ J 4 3 2
                     ♣ A J 6
   ♠ 8                                    ♠ 10 7 6
   ♡ Q 10 8 7 2          N                ♡ A 4
   ◇ A K 10 8 5     W         E           ◇ Q 9
   ♣ K 2                      S           ♣ 10 9 7 5 4 3
                     ♠ K Q J 5 2
                     ♡ J 9 6 3
                     ◇ 7 6
                     ♣ Q 8
```

West	North	East	South
	1◇	pass	1♠
pass	2♠	pass	4♠(!)
all pass			

Opening lead: ♡7

Something had to give when, at rubber bridge, Unlucky Louie cut the player we call Harlow the Halo. Harlow's luck is as consistently good as Louie's is uniformly rotten.

On the first deal, the Halo claimed a game after two finesses worked and a key suit split 3-3. Alas, the deal had to be cancelled when it was found that Louie's dummy had only twelve cards and a defender held fourteen.

Then came this deal. It's a mystery why West led a heart against four spades instead of a high diamond; but Harlow happily played low from dummy, and East took the ace and led the queen of diamonds (not best). West won the next diamond and led another heart to dummy's king.

The Halo led a trump to his king and returned the queen of clubs: king, ace. He next cashed the queen of trumps but finally ran out of luck when West discarded. Harlow then tried to ruff a heart in dummy, but East overruffed for the setting trick.

'Unlucky to go down,' Harlow shrugged. Louie rolled his eyes.

Harlow's play didn't quite match his luck. After he takes the second high trump, he can cash the jack of clubs and ruff a club. When West discards, South knows his distribution was 1-5-5-2. South then leads the jack of trumps at the tenth trick.

If West keeps one diamond and two hearts, South overtakes the jack of trumps with the ace and ruffs a diamond; dummy is good. If instead West keeps a heart and two diamonds, South lets the jack of trumps win. He ruffs a heart, and his hand is good.

8. July 7

South dealer
N-S vulnerable

```
                      ♠ A 5 3 2
                      ♡ 10 3
                      ◊ 7 4 2
                      ♣ A J 10 8
   ♠ 10 8 7 4                        ♠ 9 6
   ♡ Q 9 6 2         N               ♡ J 5
   ◊ 10 9 8     W         E          ◊ 6 5 3
   ♣ 5 3             S               ♣ Q 9 7 6 4 2
                      ♠ K Q J
                      ♡ A K 8 7 4
                      ◊ A K Q J
                      ♣ K
```

West	North	East	South
			2♣
pass	3♣	pass	3♡
pass	3♠	pass	6NT
all pass			

Opening lead: ◊ 10

It was almost midnight when my phone rang. I groped for the receiver and heard Unlucky Louie's voice.

'How nice of you to call,' I mumbled. 'What's the problem?'

'A slam I played,' Louie croaked. 'It's given me such a headache I even contacted my acupuncturist.'

'Could he see you at this hour?'

'He said to take two thumbtacks and call him in the morning. You're my only chance for any sleep.'

Louie had won the first diamond, unblocked the K-Q-J of spades and led a low heart. East took the jack and led another diamond, and Louie cashed the diamonds, overtook the king of clubs with the ace and took the ace of spades.

'I make it if hearts break 3-3,' Louie said, 'or if a defender holds four or more hearts plus the queen of clubs, since he's squeezed. As it was, I went down.'

'Your play was fine,' I said. 'It's not worth insomnia.'

'But I don't see any way to make 6NT,' Louie moaned, 'and I know there must be one.'

Can you make the slam?

South overtakes the king of clubs with the ace at the second trick and leads the jack. East takes the queen (to duck won't help) and returns a diamond. South takes three diamonds and the K-Q of spades, overtakes the jack of spades with the ace and cashes the jack of clubs at Trick 10.

Dummy has a low spade and two hearts, and South has the A-K-8 of hearts. Since West must keep the ten of spades, he can hold only two hearts, and South's eight wins the last trick. (Other winning lines are possible.)

9. July 11   Romancing the Queen

South dealer
Both vulnerable

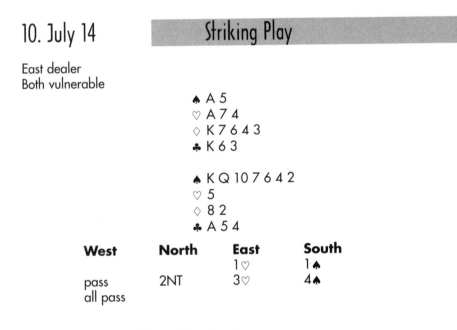

♠ Q
♡ K 8 4
◇ Q J 10 6 5
♣ A Q 10 4

West	North	East	South
			1♠
dbl	all pass		

You're West. What is your opening lead?

10. July 14   Striking Play

East dealer
Both vulnerable

♠ A 5
♡ A 7 4
◇ K 7 6 4 3
♣ K 6 3

♠ K Q 10 7 6 4 2
♡ 5
◇ 8 2
♣ A 5 4

West	North	East	South
		1♡	1♠
pass	2NT	3♡	4♠
all pass			

West leads the deuce of hearts. Plan the play.

11. July 18   Minnie's Money Game

South dealer
N-S vulnerable

```
          ♠ J 10 6
          ♡ 10 4
          ◇ A K Q J 2
          ♣ 9 8 5

          ♠ A 9 5
          ♡ A Q 9 8
          ◇ 9 7 4
          ♣ A Q 6
```

West	North	East	South
			1NT
pass	3NT	all pass	

You're declarer in a rubber-bridge game for big money. West leads the four of clubs, and you take East's jack with the queen, lead a diamond to dummy and return the ten of hearts: deuce, eight, king. West returns the king of clubs to your ace. How do you continue? (Each overtrick you win means more money.)

12. July 22   Take the Credit

North dealer
N-S vulnerable

```
          ♠ Q 10 7 6
          ♡ K 8
          ◇ A 7 4
          ♣ A K 5 2

          ♠ A K 9 8 4
          ♡ J
          ◇ K 6 3
          ♣ 9 8 4 3
```

West	North	East	South
	1NT	pass	3♠
pass	4♠	all pass	

West leads the four of hearts, and East takes the queen and leads the ace. You ruff, draw trumps in three rounds and lead a club to the ace. East drops the ten. How do you continue?

9. July 11

South dealer
Both vulnerable

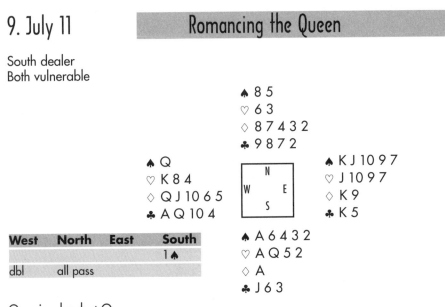

♠ 8 5
♡ 6 3
◇ 8 7 4 3 2
♣ 9 8 7 2

♠ Q
♡ K 8 4
◇ Q J 10 6 5
♣ A Q 10 4

♠ K J 10 9 7
♡ J 10 9 7
◇ K 9
♣ K 5

West	North	East	South
			1♠
dbl	all pass		

♠ A 6 4 3 2
♡ A Q 5 2
◇ A
♣ J 6 3

Opening lead: ♠Q

'I held the queen alone and didn't know what to do,' a player at the club told us.

'It all depends on what time the king is expected home,' someone else cracked.

West must have thought the king of trumps was away for the weekend since he embraced the queen and instead led the queen of diamonds against one spade doubled.

'I know you should lead trumps when partner passes your takeout double at the level of one,' West mumbled, 'but I hated to lead the queen.'

South won and led a low heart. East took the seven and shifted to trumps, but South grabbed the ace, cashed the ace of hearts and ruffed a heart. He ruffed a diamond and cashed the queen of hearts for his sixth trick, losing only 200 points.

At the other table of the match, West apparently thought the king of trumps was due home any minute: he led the queen of trumps against the same contract, and East overtook with the king. South got his three aces but was down four for a loss of 1100 points.

Bidding Quiz

YOU HOLD: ♠ A 6 4 3 2 ♡ A Q 5 2 ◇ A ♣ J 6 3. You open one spade, your partner bids 1 NT, you next bid two hearts and he returns to two spades. The opponents pass. What do you say?

ANSWER: Pass. Partner is sure to have only a doubleton spade. If instead he held three spades, he'd have raised to two spades at his first turn. Since he also promises no more than 9 points, your chances for game are next to zero.

Striking Play

East dealer
Both vulnerable

```
                              ♠ A 5
                              ♡ A 7 4
                              ◇ K 7 6 4 3
                              ♣ K 6 3
        ♠ J 9 8 3                              ♠ —
        ♡ J 8 2          N                     ♡ K Q 10 9 6 3
        ◇ 10 9 5       W     E                 ◇ A Q J
        ♣ Q 10 8          S                    ♣ J 9 7 2
                              ♠ K Q 10 7 6 4 2
                              ♡ 5
                              ◇ 8 2
                              ♣ A 5 4
```

West	North	East	South
		1♡	1♠
pass	2NT	3♡	4♠
all pass			

Opening lead: ♡2

Unlucky Louie says when his ship finally comes in, there'll be a dockworkers strike. But after this deal, North wanted to strike Louie.

Louie took the ace of hearts and cashed the ace of trumps. 'Naturally,' he sighed when East discarded.

Louie next took the K-Q of trumps and led a diamond, ducking in dummy since he knew East had the ace. East took the jack and led a heart. Louie ruffed and ducked another diamond, but East won with the queen, and Louie also lost a trump and a club.

Louie can afford a trump loser but needs to set up the diamonds for a club discard; he should lead a diamond from dummy at Trick 2. If East returns a club, Louie takes the ace and cashes the king of trumps.

If both defenders followed, Louie could draw trumps and claim. But when East discards, Louie ducks a second diamond, wins the next club in dummy and ruffs a diamond. He returns a trump to the ace and throws a club on a good diamond, losing two diamonds and a trump.

Bidding Quiz

YOU HOLD: ♠ A 5 ♡ A 7 4 ◇ K 7 6 4 3 ♣ K 6 3. With both vulnerable, the dealer, on your right, opens one heart. What do you say?

ANSWER: This is an attractive hand, with 14 good points, but you can't double with poor support for the other major suit, and you lack the strength to bid 1NT. An overcall in diamonds on a flimsy suit at the two-level begs for trouble and has little to gain since game in diamonds is far away. Pass.

Minnie's Money Game

South dealer
N-S vulnerable

```
              ♠ J 10 6
              ♡ 10 4
              ◇ A K Q J 2
              ♣ 9 8 5
♠ 7 2                      ♠ K Q 8 4 3
♡ K J 7 5         N        ♡ 6 3 2
◇ 10 5        W       E    ◇ 8 6 3
♣ K 10 7 4 3      S        ♣ J 2
              ♠ A 9 5
              ♡ A Q 9 8
              ◇ 9 7 4
              ♣ A Q 6
```

West	North	East	South
			1NT
pass	3NT	all pass	

Opening lead: ♣4

I got to the club this afternoon and was surprised to see Minnie Bottoms playing in the penny Chicago game.

'She missed the morning duplicate because of a dental appointment,' a kibitzer whispered. 'She said she feels lucky today.'

Minnie and her old bifocals, which make her confuse kings and jacks, were unknown quantities to our Chicago players. I watched as Minnie led a club against 3NT, and South took the queen and set about making as many overtricks as possible. (After all, this was for money.) He led a diamond to dummy and let the ten of hearts ride. Minnie, peering through the mist, won with the king and led the king of clubs.

South won, led a diamond to dummy and returned another heart. He had ten tricks but saw no reason not to take eleven: he took the 'proven' heart finesse with the nine. You should have heard the uproar when Minnie produced the jack and ran the clubs to beat the contract.

It was her lucky day all right; she wound up winning $65!

Bidding Quiz

YOU HOLD: ♠ 7 2 ♡ K J 7 5 ◇ 10 5 ♣ K 10 7 4 3. Your partner opens one club, and the next player bids one spade. What do you say?

ANSWER: You'd like to show the hearts, but you need more values to bid a new suit at the two-level. Bid two clubs. If your partnership uses 'negative doubles,' you can double to show this hand; but since the next player may be about to compete in spades, the descriptive club raise may work well in any case.

12. July 22

North dealer
N-S vulnerable

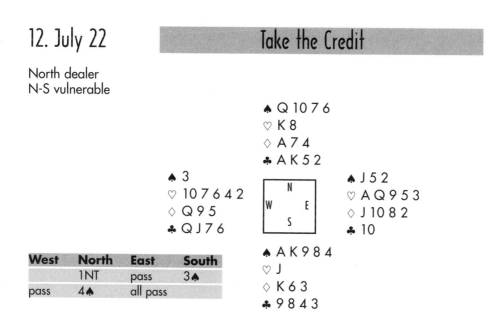

♠ Q 10 7 6
♡ K 8
♢ A 7 4
♣ A K 5 2

♠ 3
♡ 10 7 6 4 2
♢ Q 9 5
♣ Q J 7 6

♠ J 5 2
♡ A Q 9 5 3
♢ J 10 8 2
♣ 10

♠ A K 9 8 4
♡ J
♢ K 6 3
♣ 9 8 4 3

West	North	East	South
	1NT	pass	3♠
pass	4♠	all pass	

Opening lead: ♡ 4

Everyone knows how to stop an elephant from charging, but Unlucky Louie isn't having much success stopping his wife.

'When she goes to the big department store in the sky,' Louie sighs, 'Visa will retire her credit card number.'

It's a good thing Louie isn't tempted to use a credit card to pay his bridge losses. As declarer in this deal, he ruffed East's ace of hearts, drew trumps and led a club to dummy's ace. He eyed East's ten worriedly — and cashed the king next. East showed out, and West got two clubs and a diamond. Down one.

I can credit Louie — if that's the proper word — with a clear misplay. When East's ten of clubs falls, Louie should guard against a 4-1 club break by taking the top diamonds and exiting with a diamond.

If East wins, he must concede a ruff-sluff. If instead West wins and leads a club honor, Louie takes the king and gets a trick with the 9-8; if instead West leads a low club, Louie plays low from dummy to assure the contract.

Bidding Quiz

YOU HOLD: ♠ A K 9 8 4 ♡ J ♢ K 6 3 ♣ 9 8 4 3. Your partner opens one heart, you bid one spade, he rebids two hearts and you try 2NT. Partner then bids three hearts. The opponents pass. What do you say?

ANSWER: Your first two bids promised about 11 points with balanced or almost balanced distribution. Since partner knew your hand, he could have jumped to four hearts but instead signed off in three hearts. Respect his judgment and pass.

13. July 25 — Handling Temptation

South dealer
Both vulnerable

```
            ♠ 9 5 4
            ♡ 7 3
            ◇ 7 5 3
            ♣ A J 10 6 3

            ♠ A 7 2
            ♡ A K 8 5
            ◇ A K Q J 10
            ♣ K
```

West	North	East	South
			2◇
pass	2NT	pass	3♡
pass	4◇	pass	5◇
all pass			

West leads the queen of hearts. Plan the play.

14. July 28 — Second Hand Rising

South dealer
Neither vulnerable

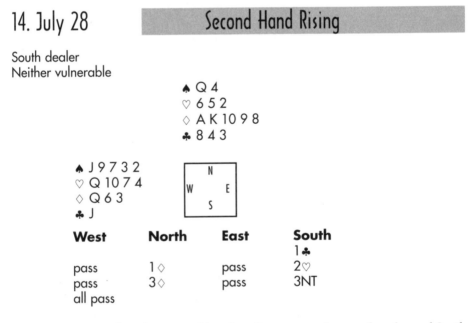

```
            ♠ Q 4
            ♡ 6 5 2
            ◇ A K 10 9 8
            ♣ 8 4 3

♠ J 9 7 3 2      N
♡ Q 10 7 4    W     E
◇ Q 6 3          S
♣ J
```

West	North	East	South
			1♣
pass	1◇	pass	2♡
pass	3◇	pass	3NT
all pass			

You lead the three of spades: queen, king, five. East returns the ten of spades, and South follows with the six. Plan the defense.

15. July 31 — Sine of the Times

North dealer
N-S vulnerable

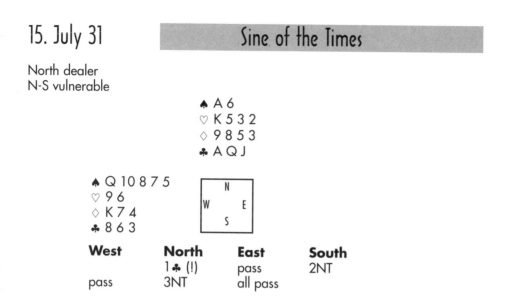

```
                    ♠ A 6
                    ♡ K 5 3 2
                    ◊ 9 8 5 3
                    ♣ A Q J

   ♠ Q 10 8 7 5         N
   ♡ 9 6           W         E
   ◊ K 7 4              S
   ♣ 8 6 3
```

West	North	East	South
	1♣ (!)	pass	2NT
pass	3NT	all pass	

You lead the seven of spades, declarer plays low from dummy and East's jack wins. Back comes the four of spades to dummy's ace. Plan the defense.

16. August 1 — Tell Me No Secrets

North dealer
E-W vulnerable

```
                    ♠ J 9 8
                    ♡ J 8 2
                    ◊ K Q 10 7 6
                    ♣ 6 3


                    ♠ A K
                    ♡ A 9 3
                    ◊ J 9 8
                    ♣ A Q J 5 2
```

West	North	East	South
	pass	pass	1♣
pass	1◊	pass	2NT
pass	3NT	all pass	

West leads the three of spades. Plan the play.

Handling Temptation

South dealer
Both vulnerable

```
                      ♠ 9 5 4
                      ♡ 7 3
                      ◊ 7 5 3
                      ♣ A J 10 6 3
   ♠ Q 8 3                          ♠ K J 10 6
   ♡ Q J 10 9 4        N            ♡ 6 2
   ◊ 6 4           W       E        ◊ 9 8 2
   ♣ Q 7 2             S            ♣ 9 8 5 4
                      ♠ A 7 2
                      ♡ A K 8 5
                      ◊ A K Q J 10
                      ♣ K
```

West	North	East	South
			2◊
pass	2NT	pass	3♡
pass	4◊	pass	5◊
all pass			

Opening lead: ♡Q

Cy the Cynic says that resisting temptation is usually just a matter of putting it off until nobody's looking. Unfortunately, there were three witnesses — four, counting a kibitzer — when Cy was declarer in this deal.

Cy took the ace and king of hearts, unblocked his king of clubs and led a third heart, ruffing in dummy. East overruffed and shifted to the jack of spades. Cy took the ace, cashed one high trump and tried to ruff his last heart in dummy. East overruffed again, and the defense took two spades. Down two.

Cy does better if he resists the temptation to ruff a heart in dummy; the chance that East will overruff is too great. Cy must instead throw a spade on the third heart as a loser-on-loser play.

If West shifts to a trump, Cy wins and leads a fourth heart, again pitching a spade from dummy. Cy can win the next trump, cash the ace of spades and safely ruff a spade in dummy. He can then throw his last spade on the ace of clubs and claim the rest.

Bidding Quiz

YOU HOLD: ♠ Q 8 3 ♡ Q J 10 9 4 ◊ 6 4 ♣ Q 7 2. Dealer, on your left, opens one heart. Your partner doubles, and the next player passes. What do you say?

ANSWER: The hearts are strong enough to pass for a penalty, but that action wouldn't appeal to me with no sure side tricks. Trade the two side queens for an ace, and I'd pass. With the actual hand, I'd play safe by bidding 1NT, promising a balanced 6 to 9 points with a heart trick.

14. July 28

Second Hand Rising

South dealer
Neither vulnerable

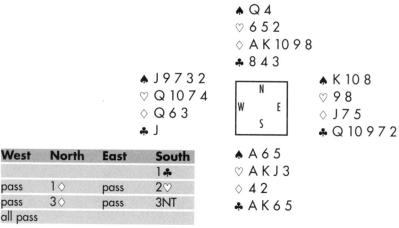

♠ Q 4
♡ 6 5 2
◇ A K 10 9 8
♣ 8 4 3

♠ J 9 7 3 2
♡ Q 10 7 4
◇ Q 6 3
♣ J

♠ K 10 8
♡ 9 8
◇ J 7 5
♣ Q 10 9 7 2

♠ A 6 5
♡ A K J 3
◇ 4 2
♣ A K 6 5

West	North	East	South
			1♣
pass	1◇	pass	2♡
pass	3◇	pass	3NT
all pass			

Opening lead: ♠3

It had been several months since my old friend Second Hand Rose had dropped by the club. When the defenders' rule about 'second hand low' was being taught, Rose must have been off on her honeymoon with Jake the plumber.

Rose led a spade against 3NT, and South put up dummy's queen hopefully. When East covered, South played low, refused the next spade and won the third spade. South then led a diamond, and Second Hand Rose... with the queen!

South was stuck. If he played low to keep a link with dummy, Rose would cash two spades to beat the contract. So South took the A-K of diamonds and tried a heart to his jack, hoping for four heart tricks, two diamonds, a spade and two clubs. Rose produced the queen, cashed her spades and led a diamond to East's jack. Down two.

If Rose plays low on the first diamond, South plays the ten from dummy, losing to East. South can win the return, lead another diamond, and take four diamonds, two hearts, two clubs and a spade.

Bidding Quiz

YOU HOLD: ♠ A 6 5 ♡ A K J 3 ◇ 4 2 ♣ A K 6 5. Dealer, on your right, opens one spade. You double, and your partner bids two diamonds. The opponents pass. What do you say?

ANSWER: You mustn't pass; since partner may have as many as 9 points, game is possible, and your diamond support isn't what it should be. Still, you shouldn't be eager to try 2NT with only a single spade stopper and no ready source of tricks. Bid two hearts.

North dealer
N-S vulnerable

```
                        ♠ A 6
                        ♡ K 5 3 2
                        ◇ 9 8 5 3
                        ♣ A Q J
  ♠ Q 10 8 7 5                        ♠ J 4 3
  ♡ 9 6              N                ♡ Q J 10 8
  ◇ K 7 4         W     E             ◇ 10 2
  ♣ 8 6 3            S                ♣ K 10 9 2
                        ♠ K 9 2
                        ♡ A 7 4
                        ◇ A Q J 6
                        ♣ 7 5 4
```

West	North	East	South
	1♣ (!)	pass	2NT
pass	3NT	all pass	

Opening lead: ♠7

'He's got more angles than a trigonometry book,' a player fumed to me about one of our trickier defenders.

'Well, don't go off on a tangent,' I said. 'Let's hear what happened.'

'We were playing a set game,' my friend said. 'As South I ducked the first spade, won the next in dummy and led a diamond to my queen. And the man played low smoothly!

'I next led a heart to the king and a diamond to my jack. Now he won and led a heart. I took the ace and tried the club finesse for my ninth trick, but East won and cashed two hearts to beat me. My partner and I wound up having to cosine a loan to pay our losses.'

West's play was as easy as pi for a good defender, who knows the benefits of keeping his entry and letting declarer win the first try at a repeatable finesse. But South has a secant chance by cashing the ace of diamonds after he takes the queen. If both defenders follow low, South forces out the king, wins the next spade and finesses in clubs. He loses a club, a diamond and at most two spades.

Bidding Quiz

YOU HOLD: ♠ K 9 2 ♡ A 7 4 ◇ A Q J 6 ♣ 7 5 4. Your partner opens one spade, you respond two diamonds, he next bids two hearts and you jump to three spades. Partner then bids four clubs. The opponents pass. What do you say?

ANSWER: Partner is interested in slam; his cuebid of four clubs suggests the ace. Since you have helping honors in his suits, go along by cuebidding four diamonds; but if he signs off in four spades next, you'll pass.

16. August 1

North dealer
E-W vulnerable

```
                    ♠ J 9 8
                    ♡ J 8 2
                    ◇ K Q 10 7 6
                    ♣ 6 3
   ♠ Q 10 7 3 2                      ♠ 6 5 4
   ♡ K 10 7 4        N              ♡ Q 6 5
   ◇ 3 2          W     E           ◇ A 5 4
   ♣ 7 4             S              ♣ K 10 9 8
                    ♠ A K
                    ♡ A 9 3
                    ◇ J 9 8
                    ♣ A Q J 5 2
```

West	North	East	South
	pass	pass	1♣
pass	1◇	pass	2NT
pass	3NT	all pass	

Opening lead: ♠3

'Can you keep a secret?' a player at the club whispered.

'Sure,' I said. 'It's the people I tell it to who can't.'

'I just saw Ed lose a contract my cat could make.'

Since Ed is a top player, I got the details. He took the king of spades and led the jack of diamonds. East ducked and ducked again when South led a diamond to the queen.

'To lead another diamond wouldn't help,' I was told; 'dummy had no entry. Ed finessed the jack of clubs and led the ace and a low club, but East took the ten and led a spade. The defense got two clubs, a diamond and three spades.'

I won't say a cat could make 3NT, but an expert can go down if he has an aberration. South must lead a diamond to the king at Trick 2 and finesse in clubs. (He needs at least two club tricks in any case.) He next overtakes the jack of diamonds with the queen, ducked. South then repeats the club finesse, cashes the ace and concedes a club. He has four clubs, two diamonds, two spades and a heart.

Bidding Quiz

YOU HOLD: ♠ 6 5 4 ♡ Q 6 5 ◇ A 5 4 ♣ K 10 9 8. Your partner opens one heart, you raise to two hearts and he next bids four clubs. The opponents pass. What do you say?

ANSWER: Partner's four clubs commits your side to game and therefore suggests interest in slam; he has a strong two-suiter. Since you have three valuable honors, you should plan to bid at least a small slam. For the moment, show your ace with a cuebid of four diamonds.

17. August 3 — Rising from the Ashes

South dealer
Both vulnerable

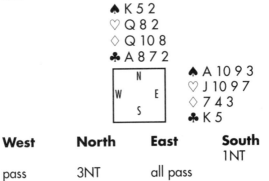

```
              ♠ K 5 2
              ♡ Q 8 2
              ◇ Q 10 8
              ♣ A 8 7 2
                              ♠ A 10 9 3
         N                    ♡ J 10 9 7
      W     E                 ◇ 7 4 3
         S                    ♣ K 5
```

West	North	East	South
			1NT
pass	3NT	all pass	

West leads the seven of spades, and dummy plays low. What do you play as East?

18. August 5 — Smarter With Age

North dealer
Neither vulnerable

```
              ♠ A 9 8 5 4
              ♡ A J
              ◇ A 10 4
              ♣ 8 6 4


              ♠ —
              ♡ Q 9 6
              ◇ K Q 8 6 5 3 2
              ♣ A 10 2
```

West	North	East	South
	1♠	pass	2◇
pass	2♠	pass	3♣
pass	4◇	pass	5♣
pass	6◇	all pass	

West leads the king of spades. Plan the play.

19. August 9

Blind Leads

North dealer
Both vulnerable

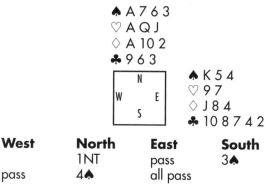

♠ A 7 6 3
♡ A Q J
◇ A 10 2
♣ 9 6 3

♠ K 5 4
♡ 9 7
◇ J 8 4
♣ 10 8 7 4 2

West	North	East	South
	1NT	pass	3♠
pass	4♠	all pass	

West leads the three of diamonds, and dummy plays low. What do you play as East?

20. August 14

Harlow Wins Again

South dealer
Both vulnerable

♠ 7 6 4
♡ A 5 4
◇ Q 4
♣ A Q 7 6 3

♠ A K 9 2
♡ K 8 7 6 2
◇ 6 5
♣ K 9

West	North	East	South
			1♡
pass	2♣	pass	2♡
pass	4♡	all pass	

West leads the ace of diamonds and another diamond to East's king. East shifts to the five of spades. Plan the play.

Rising from the Ashes

South dealer
Both vulnerable

```
                            ♠ K 5 2
                            ♡ Q 8 2
                            ◇ Q 10 8
                            ♣ A 8 7 2
        ♠ Q J 8 7                         ♠ A 10 9 3
        ♡ 6 4            N                ♡ J 10 9 7
        ◇ 9 6 5 2    W       E            ◇ 7 4 3
        ♣ 6 4 3          S                ♣ K 5
                            ♠ 6 4
                            ♡ A K 5 3
                            ◇ A K J
                            ♣ Q J 10 9
```

West	North	East	South
			1NT
pass	3NT	all pass	

Opening lead: ♠7

'I've never played this badly before,' East sighed. Alas for him, West was Grapefruit, the member of my club with an acid disposition.

'You've played before?' was Grapefruit's comment.

Grapefruit had led the seven of spades against 3NT. Dummy played low, and East stewed, took the ace and returned the ten. South refused the trick, won the next spade, led a heart to his hand and returned the queen of clubs to finesse. East won and cashed one spade, but South took the rest.

Assuming West's seven was his fourth-best spade, East could tell South had no higher spades; hence East could play the three on the first spade. West would lead the queen next, and the defense would take four spades and a club.

Some players are known by the silence they keep — but not Grapefruit. 'Exactly what time today did you learn to play?' he asked East.

East listened calmly; and then, just as calmly, he picked up an overflowing ashtray and dumped its contents on Grapefruit's head!

Bidding Quiz

YOU HOLD: ♠ A 10 9 3 ♡ J 10 9 7 ◇ 7 4 3 ♣ K 5. Your partner opens two clubs (strong, artificial), you respond two diamonds (waiting), he bids two hearts, you raise to three hearts and he bids four clubs. What do you say?

ANSWER: Partner's four clubs is a cuebid, looking for slam and promising the ace. Since all your values look good, you must cooperate. Bid four spades to show your ace. If partner bids five diamonds next, you'll try six clubs to show the king and suggest a grand slam.

18. August 5

North dealer
Neither vulnerable

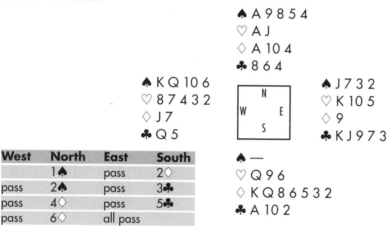

```
                    ♠ A 9 8 5 4
                    ♡ A J
                    ◇ A 10 4
                    ♣ 8 6 4
      ♠ K Q 10 6                    ♠ J 7 3 2
      ♡ 8 7 4 3 2      N            ♡ K 10 5
      ◇ J 7         W     E         ◇ 9
      ♣ Q 5            S            ♣ K J 9 7 3
                    ♠ —
                    ♡ Q 9 6
                    ◇ K Q 8 6 5 3 2
                    ♣ A 10 2
```

West	North	East	South
	1♠	pass	2◇
pass	2♠	pass	3♣
pass	4◇	pass	5♣
pass	6◇	all pass	

Opening lead: ♠K

'You know,' said Unlucky Louie, 'I've heard that a man reaches the peak of his intelligence at age forty-seven.'

'Just when there are fewer people around the house to listen to him,' I smiled. 'By the way, isn't your birthday next week?'

'That has nothing to do with it,' Louie growled, 'but it's true I'm playing better.'

Louie showed me this deal; he and North did well to reach a 24-point slam. How would you play when West leads the king of spades?

'I counted twelve tricks if the heart finesse won,' Louie said, 'but for an extra chance, I played low from dummy on the first spade and ruffed in my hand. I led a trump to the ace, ruffed a spade, drew trumps and tried a heart to the jack.

'East won and led a club, and I took the ace, led a heart to the ace, threw a club on the ace of spades and ruffed a spade. When spades broke 4-4, I ruffed my queen of hearts in dummy and threw my last club on the good spade.'

Louie played it well. Maybe he's getting luckier with age.

Bidding Quiz

YOU HOLD: ♠ A 9 8 5 4 ♡ A J ◇ A 10 4 ♣ 8 6 4. Your partner opens one diamond, you bid one spade, he jumps to three clubs and you return to three diamonds. Partner next bids 3NT. What do you say?

ANSWER: Don't stop below slam. Partner's jump promised at least 19 points (enough for game even if you'd had a minimum response with 6 points), and you have 13 points. With most partners, forget science; just bid six diamonds or 6NT.

19. August 9

North dealer
Both vulnerable

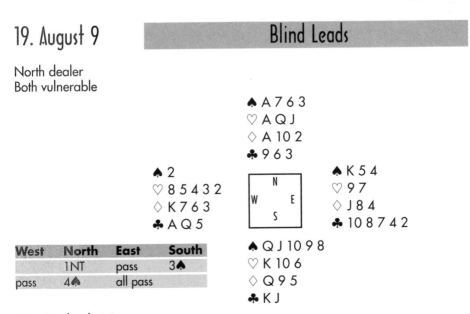

```
                    ♠ A 7 6 3
                    ♡ A Q J
                    ◇ A 10 2
                    ♣ 9 6 3
  ♠ 2                              ♠ K 5 4
  ♡ 8 5 4 3 2          N           ♡ 9 7
  ◇ K 7 6 3        W     E         ◇ J 8 4
  ♣ A Q 5             S            ♣ 10 8 7 4 2
                    ♠ Q J 10 9 8
                    ♡ K 10 6
                    ◇ Q 9 5
                    ♣ K J
```

West	North	East	South
	1NT	pass	3♠
pass	4♠	all pass	

Opening lead: ◇3

Cy the Cynic has had so many blind dates he should qualify for a free guide dog. Unlucky Louie fixed him up with a cousin who happened to play bridge.

'Dinner went fine,' Cy told me, 'and so did the bridge until this deal. My date led a diamond against four spades. Dummy played low, and my jack lost to the queen. South lost the trump finesse, and I next led a club. My partner took two clubs, but South ruffed the third club, drew trumps and led a diamond to the ten to make the game.'

'I told my date she shouldn't have led an aggressive diamond from the king when North had shown a balanced hand. She said it had been a blind lead, and I was a result merchant. When I took her home, she didn't ask me in.'

I fear it was a case of the blind date leading the blind. Perhaps West's diamond lead was unwise, but Cy goofed by playing his jack: since South was marked with an honor, Cy must instead play the eight. South takes the nine but later loses a diamond for down one.

Bidding Quiz

YOU HOLD: ♠ 2 ♡ 8 5 4 3 2 ◇ K 7 6 3 ♣ A Q 5. Your partner opens one diamond, you respond one heart and he next bids one spade. The opponents pass. What do you say?

ANSWER: Most pairs use second-round jumps by responder to invite game, not to force. Otherwise, a hand such as this is hard to describe. If that's your agreement, bid three diamonds. But if a jump to three diamonds would be forcing, you must underbid substantially with two diamonds.

Harlow Wins Again

South dealer
Both vulnerable

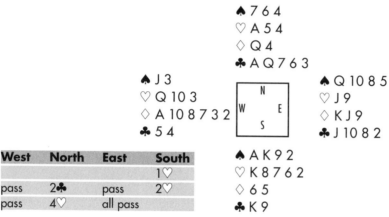

```
              ♠ 7 6 4
              ♡ A 5 4
              ◇ Q 4
              ♣ A Q 7 6 3
♠ J 3                        ♠ Q 10 8 5
♡ Q 10 3        N            ♡ J 9
◇ A 10 8 7 3 2  W    E       ◇ K J 9
♣ 5 4              S         ♣ J 10 8 2
              ♠ A K 9 2
              ♡ K 8 7 6 2
              ◇ 6 5
              ♣ K 9
```

West	North	East	South
			1♡
pass	2♣	pass	2♡
pass	4♡	all pass	

Opening lead: ◇A

Harlow the Halo flourishes in my club like a weed in a hothouse. While Unlucky Louie's key suits break 5-0, Harlow attracts good luck like flies to honey.

Moreover, his errors go unpunished. Louie, East, won the second diamond and led a spade. Harlow won, took the K-A of clubs and ruffed a club with his deuce of trumps. West overruffed and led another spade, but Harlow won, drew trumps with the king and ace, and threw his low spades on the good clubs.

'He's got more luck than the phone company's got wrong numbers,' sighed Louie.

West has a chance if he doesn't overruff on the third club. Harlow can still succeed by cashing a second spade before taking the king and ace of trumps; then if West ruffs the queen of clubs next, he's endplayed. But Harlow does best to ruff the third club with the six of trumps. If West discards, Harlow takes the king, leads the seven to the ace and discards a spade on the queen of clubs.

West ruffs, but Harlow can reach dummy with the five of trumps to pitch his last spade on the last club.

Bidding Quiz

YOU HOLD: ♠ A K 9 2 ♡ K 8 7 6 2 ◇ 6 5 ♣ K 9. Dealer, on your right, opens one diamond. What do you say?

ANSWER: Experts once doubled on hands such as this, but back then they also overcalled with skinny values. A double might cause trouble: if partner responded two clubs, the hand wouldn't be strong enough to bid hearts next; hence you might lose a 5-3 heart fit. Bid one heart. If partner has spades, he may bid the suit over one heart.

21. August 18 — Marriage in Spades

South dealer
N-S vulnerable

```
            ♠ A J 10 4
            ♡ 5 3
            ◇ J 7 3
            ♣ Q 7 4 3

            ♠ 6 5 2
            ♡ A K Q J 7 2
            ◇ A 2
            ♣ A 2
```

West	North	East	South
			1♡
1♠	1NT	pass	4♡
all pass			

West leads the king of spades. Plan the play.

22. August 20 — A Galling Display

North dealer
Neither vulnerable

```
            ♠ K 6 3
            ♡ K 10 8 5
            ◇ A K 6
            ♣ K 6 2

            ♠ 7 4
            ♡ A J 9 6 4 2
            ◇ 9 4
            ♣ A J 5
```

West	North	East	South
	1NT	pass	4♡
all pass			

West leads the queen of spades and continues spades. You ruff the third spade. How do you play the trumps?

23. August 25 — Matter of Fact

East dealer
Both vulnerable

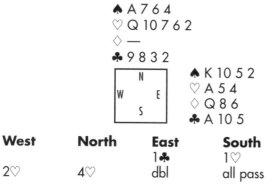

♠ A 7 6 4
♡ Q 10 7 6 2
♢ —
♣ 9 8 3 2

♠ K 10 5 2
♡ A 5 4
♢ Q 8 6
♣ A 10 5

West	North	East	South
		1♣	1♡
2♡	4♡	dbl	all pass

West leads the king of clubs, and declarer plays low from dummy. Plan the defense.

24. September 2 — Louie's Good News

South dealer
Both vulnerable

♠ K Q
♡ 10 2
♢ K 6 3
♣ A K 9 8 5 4

♠ 9 5 4 2
♡ A K Q J 9 8
♢ A
♣ 7 3

West	North	East	South
			1♡
pass	2♣	pass	4♡
pass	4NT	pass	5♡
pass	6♡	all pass	

West leads the queen of diamonds. Plan the play.

21. August 18

South dealer
N-S vulnerable

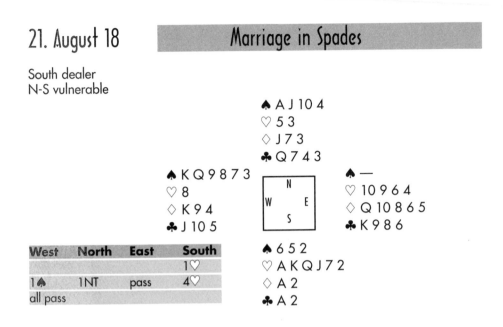

```
                         ♠ A J 10 4
                         ♡ 5 3
                         ◇ J 7 3
                         ♣ Q 7 4 3
         ♠ K Q 9 8 7 3        ┌─────┐        ♠ —
         ♡ 8                   │  N  │        ♡ 10 9 6 4
         ◇ K 9 4              W│     │E       ◇ Q 10 8 6 5
         ♣ J 10 5             │  S  │        ♣ K 9 8 6
                              └─────┘
                         ♠ 6 5 2
                         ♡ A K Q J 7 2
                         ◇ A 2
                         ♣ A 2
```

West	North	East	South
			1♡
1♠	1NT	pass	4♡
all pass			

Opening lead: ♠K

I got to the club just before a team match and found Cy the Cynic, a confirmed bachelor, debating the virtues of wedded life with Wendy the Feminist.

'A man's just not complete until he's married,' Wendy was saying.

'True,' Cy nodded, 'and then he's totally finished.'

'Don't you know any good marriages?' Wendy demanded.

'Adam and Eve had one,' Cy said solemnly. 'He couldn't talk about his mother's cooking, and she couldn't bring up the men she could have married.'

It was match time, so Cy escaped with only a poke in the ribs. On the first deal I watched, Cy, West, didn't hesitate to break up his marriage in spades: he led the king against Wendy's contract of four hearts. Dummy played the ace, and East ruffed and led a diamond.

Wendy took the ace, drew trumps and led a spade. Cy played low, of course, and Wendy won in dummy and lost a diamond. She ruffed the next diamond and led another spade, but this time Cy took his queen, and Wendy lost a club. Down one.

'Cold as ice,' I told Cy later. 'Wendy plays low from dummy on the first spade and the ten on the next spade. East ruffs and leads a diamond, but Wendy wins, draws trumps and finesses with the jack of spades for her tenth trick.'

Cy shrugged. 'Wendy still doesn't realize she goofed, but I never try to change a woman's mind; it's better to give her the satisfaction of doing it for herself.'

'Besides,' Cy went on, 'Wendy can play however she wants. She has a perfect right. And also a pretty good left.'

22. August 20

North dealer
Neither vulnerable

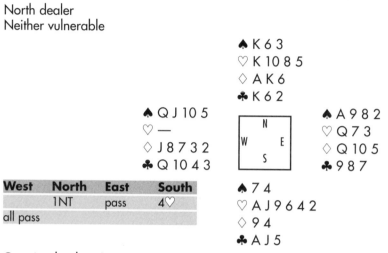

```
              ♠ K 6 3
              ♡ K 10 8 5
              ◇ A K 6
              ♣ K 6 2
♠ Q J 10 5              ♠ A 9 8 2
♡ —          N         ♡ Q 7 3
◇ J 8 7 3 2  W    E    ◇ Q 10 5
♣ Q 10 4 3      S      ♣ 9 8 7
              ♠ 7 4
              ♡ A J 9 6 4 2
              ◇ 9 4
              ♣ A J 5
```

West	North	East	South
	1NT	pass	4♡
all pass			

Opening lead: ♠Q

Grapefruit, our member who owns and operates an acid disposition, had to go back to the hospital after another attack of gallstones.

'Last time they got the stones,' Unlucky Louie observed. 'Maybe this time they'll remove some of his gall.'

Grapefruit was at the club — and in rare form — the day he took ill. As North, he watched South ruff the third spade and cash the ace of trumps and then the king. South next lost a club finesse with the jack. East got a trump trick, and Grapefruit told South that if his brains were money, he'd have to float a loan to buy a pack of gum.

South protested that he'd had to guess which high trump to cash first. What do you think?

South must start the trumps by taking the king. He can then pick up East's queen and lose one club when the finesse fails. If instead West had all three missing trumps, South would continue with the ace of trumps, the A-K of diamonds and a diamond ruff. He would then lead a trump to endplay West.

Bidding Quiz

YOU HOLD: ♠ A 9 8 2 ♡ Q 7 3 ◇ Q 10 5 ♣ 9 8 7. Your partner opens one heart, you raise to two hearts and he next bids four diamonds. The opponents pass. What do you say?

ANSWER: When partner bid four diamonds, he committed to game without simply bidding game; hence he's interested in slam and has a powerful two-suited hand such as ♠ 4 ♡ A K J 6 5 ◇ A K 9 7 6 ♣ A 4. Since all of your honors will be useful, you should cooperate. Cuebid four spades to get partner's reaction.

23. August 25

East dealer
Both vulnerable

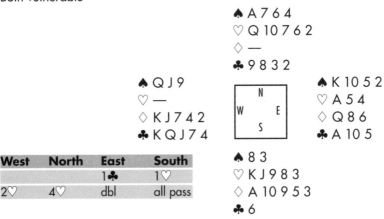

♠ A 7 6 4
♡ Q 10 7 6 2
◇ —
♣ 9 8 3 2

♠ Q J 9
♡ —
◇ K J 7 4 2
♣ K Q J 7 4

♠ K 10 5 2
♡ A 5 4
◇ Q 8 6
♣ A 10 5

♠ 8 3
♡ K J 9 8 3
◇ A 10 9 5 3
♣ 6

West	North	East	South
		1♣	1♡
2♡	4♡	dbl	all pass

Opening lead: ♣K

Cy the Cynic, who is always sure about things that are a matter of opinion, had quite a tiff with East after this deal.

Cy's king of clubs won, and he shifted to the queen of spades. South took the ace, ruffed a club, cashed the ace of diamonds, ruffed a diamond, ruffed a club and ruffed a diamond. He next led dummy's last club, and when East discarded, South threw his last spade.

Cy won and still couldn't lead a trump. He tried the jack of diamonds, and South ruffed with dummy's ten. East overruffed and led a trump, but South won and crossruffed the last three tricks, scoring 790 points.

Cy told East he had no business doubling four hearts.

'I didn't want to hear you bid five clubs,' East protested.

'Everyone's entitled to my opinion,' Cy cut him off.

There's room for opinion about the bidding, but East should defeat four hearts. His easiest defense is to overtake the king of clubs to shift to the ace and a low trump. South's crossruff comes up a trick short.

Bidding Quiz

YOU HOLD: ♠ K 10 5 2 ♡ A 5 4 ◇ Q 8 6 ♣ A 10 5. Dealer, on your right, opens one heart. What do you say?

ANSWER: Opinion differs on hands of this type, but I'd pass and I believe a slight majority of experts would prefer that action. This hand looks better for defending. The alternative call is a takeout double, but if your partner's hand is weak, you'll be headed for a minus score — possibly a large one.

24. September 2 Louie's Good News

South dealer
Both vulnerable

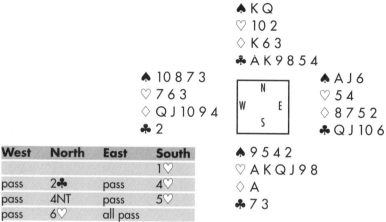

♠ K Q
♡ 10 2
◇ K 6 3
♣ A K 9 8 5 4

♠ 10 8 7 3
♡ 7 6 3
◇ Q J 10 9 4
♣ 2

♠ A J 6
♡ 5 4
◇ 8 7 5 2
♣ Q J 10 6

♠ 9 5 4 2
♡ A K Q J 9 8
◇ A
♣ 7 3

West	North	East	South
			1♡
pass	2♣	pass	4♡
pass	4NT	pass	5♡
pass	6♡	all pass	

Opening lead: ◇Q

'It was a good-news-bad-news situation,' Unlucky Louie said, showing me the deal for today.

'West didn't lead a trump against my six hearts,' Louie told me, 'so I could ruff a spade in dummy. When I led a spade to the king at the second trick, East won and led a trump. I won, took the queen of spades, ruffed a diamond, ruffed a spade and threw my last spade on the king of diamonds.

'The good news was that I had twelve tricks; the bad news was that dummy had only clubs left. When I led the ace and king, West ruffed.'

If Louie ever won a raffle, the prize would be a cruise on the Titanic. 'Do you think your play was best?' I asked him.

'If I try to set up the clubs,' he shrugged, 'the 4-1 break still beats me.'

Louie must lead a club to dummy at Trick 2 and pitch his other low club on the king of diamonds. He ruffs a club, returns a trump to dummy's ten and ruffs a club. Louie can then draw trumps and lead a spade, eventually reaching dummy to discard spades on the good clubs.

Bidding Quiz

YOU HOLD: ♠ K Q ♡ 10 2 ◇ K 6 3 ♣ A K 9 8 5 4. You open one club, and your partner bids one heart. The opponents pass. What do you say?

ANSWER: This decision is close, but since the rules won't let you rebid two and a half clubs, you must pick between a timid two clubs and an aggressive three clubs. Since the value of your doubleton spade honors decreases, I'd settle for two clubs. With K-9 in spades and A-K-Q-8-5-4 in clubs, I'd try three clubs.

PART 4

Fall

1. September 6 — Monkey On His Back

South dealer
Both vulnerable

```
              ♠ K 9 7 3
              ♡ K Q 10
              ◇ 10 9 8
              ♣ A 6 5

              ♠ A 8
              ♡ A 9 7
              ◇ A K Q
              ♣ K J 10 8 7
```

West	North	East	South
			2NT
pass	6NT	all pass	

West leads the seven of diamonds. Plan the play.

2. September 8 — Minnie's Hearing Aid

South dealer
N-S vulnerable

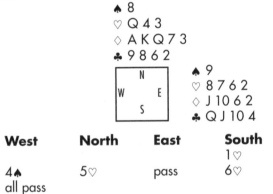

```
              ♠ 8
              ♡ Q 4 3
              ◇ A K Q 7 3
              ♣ 9 8 6 2
                              ♠ 9
                              ♡ 8 7 6 2
                              ◇ J 10 6 2
                              ♣ Q J 10 4
```

West	North	East	South
			1♡
4♠	5♡	pass	6♡
all pass			

West leads the king of spades and then the ace. Declarer ruffs with dummy's queen of trumps. What do you discard?

3. September 10   Helping Yourself

South dealer
Both vulnerable

     ♠ Q J 5 4
     ♡ K 9 8 4
     ◇ 10 8 4
     ♣ 9 5

     ♠ K 10
     ♡ A Q J 10 6 3
     ◇ J 7 2
     ♣ A Q

West	North	East	South
			1♡
dbl	2♡	pass	4♡
all pass			

West leads the deuce of clubs. Do you see any chance for the contract?

4. September 13   From My Archives

West dealer
N-S vulnerable

     ♠ A J 8 5
     ♡ A 7 6 2
     ◇ Q 3
     ♣ A J 9

              ♠ Q 10 7 2
   N   ♡ K Q 9 8
W   E   ◇ K 10
   S   ♣ Q 10 8

West	North	East	South
1◇	dbl	redbl	2♣
pass	pass	dbl	all pass

West leads the jack of hearts. Dummy plays low, and West leads a second heart. Declarer takes the ace and leads a diamond from dummy, and your ten wins. Plan the defense.

1. September 6

South dealer
Both vulnerable

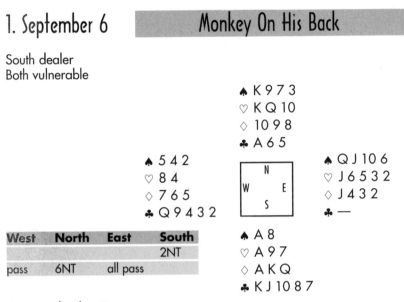

```
                    ♠ K 9 7 3
                    ♡ K Q 10
                    ◇ 10 9 8
                    ♣ A 6 5
    ♠ 5 4 2                         ♠ Q J 10 6
    ♡ 8 4            N              ♡ J 6 5 3 2
    ◇ 7 6 5     W        E          ◇ J 4 3 2
    ♣ Q 9 4 3 2     S              ♣ —
                    ♠ A 8
                    ♡ A 9 7
                    ◇ A K Q
                    ♣ K J 10 8 7
```

West	North	East	South
			2NT
pass	6NT	all pass	

Opening lead: ◇7

'Show me a monkey banging on a typewriter,' Unlucky Louie said. 'I could bet against his writing a book, and in a week he'd have a contract with Simon and Schuster.'

'What now?' I sighed.

'I led a club to dummy's ace at the second trick,' Louie said. 'If clubs broke 3-2 or 4-1, I might lose one club, but that'd be all. Even if all five clubs lay on my right, I'd win four club tricks. I'd make the slam 49 times out of 50, but when he showed out at my right, I lost two clubs.'

'Tough luck,' I agreed; but Louie can always make the slam by leading the jack of clubs at Trick 2, letting it ride if West plays low. If East can win, Louie has the rest. As the cards actually lie, he leads a second club through West to assure four club tricks. If West shows out on the first club, Louie takes the ace and returns a club from dummy, winning four clubs.

Actually, Louie can get home after leading a club to the ace (by endplaying West), but the safety play guarantees the slam.

Bidding Quiz

YOU HOLD: ♠ K 9 7 3 ♡ K Q 10 ◇ 10 9 8 ♣ A 6 5. Your partner opens one diamond, you bid one spade, he rebids two diamonds and you try 2NT. Partner next bids three clubs. The opponents pass. What do you say?

ANSWER: Bid three diamonds. Partner suggests six diamonds, four clubs and a minimum hand. Your second bid was conservative, but you can't change your mind and insist on 3NT now, especially when partner warns against that contract.

Minnie's Hearing Aid

South dealer
N-S vulnerable

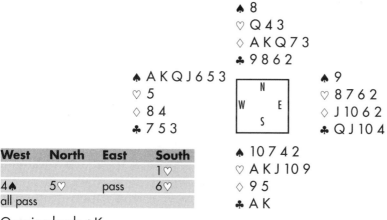

```
                         ♠ 8
                         ♡ Q 4 3
                         ◊ A K Q 7 3
                         ♣ 9 8 6 2
        ♠ A K Q J 6 5 3              ♠ 9
        ♡ 5             ┌───────┐    ♡ 8 7 6 2
        ◊ 8 4          │   N   │    ◊ J 10 6 2
        ♣ 7 5 3        │ W   E │    ♣ Q J 10 4
                        │   S   │
                        └───────┘
                         ♠ 10 7 4 2
                         ♡ A K J 10 9
                         ◊ 9 5
                         ♣ A K
```

West	North	East	South
			1♡
4♠	5♡	pass	6♡
all pass			

Opening lead: ♠K

'Minnie gets me because she can't see well enough to tell kings from jacks,' Cy the Cynic said bitterly, 'and she gets me because she won't buy a hearing aid. If taste and smell were factors, I'd have no chance at all.'

Cy, with the club's senior member Minnie Bottoms on his right, reached this slam in a duplicate game. When West led two high spades, Cy called for dummy's queen of trumps.

'If Minnie throws a diamond,' Cy told me, 'I draw trumps and run the diamonds; if she throws a club, I draw trumps, cash the top clubs, lead a diamond to dummy and ruff a club to set up the fourth club for my twelfth trick.'

'So what was the problem?' I asked, though I could already see.

'She underruffed!' Cy said. 'She thought she'd heard me call for the three of trumps, not the queen, and was taking the setting trick. I was dead anyway. When I drew trumps, she could discard after the dummy.'

'Maybe she's better off without a hearing aid,' I said innocently.

Bidding Quiz

YOU HOLD: ♠ 10 7 4 2 ♡ A K J 10 9 ◊ 9 5 ♣ A K. Your partner opens one diamond, you bid one heart and he bids two clubs. The opponents pass. What do you say?

ANSWER: Since partner's strength and pattern are still unclear, you can't place the contract. Force with a bid of two spades. If partner next bids 2NT, you'll raise to 3NT; if he rebids a minor suit, you'll bid three hearts, promising six hearts or five very strong hearts.

3. September 10

South dealer
Both vulnerable

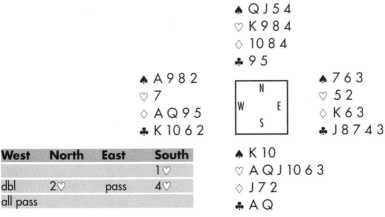

♠ Q J 5 4
♡ K 9 8 4
◇ 10 8 4
♣ 9 5

♠ A 9 8 2
♡ 7
◇ A Q 9 5
♣ K 10 6 2

♠ 7 6 3
♡ 5 2
◇ K 6 3
♣ J 8 7 4 3

♠ K 10
♡ A Q J 10 6 3
◇ J 7 2
♣ A Q

West	North	East	South
			1♡
dbl	2♡	pass	4♡
all pass			

Opening lead: ♣2

'Ever heard of Brigidda?' Cy the Cynic asked us.

'Who's he?' Unlucky Louie wanted to know.

'It's a she,' Cy said: 'the goddess of fate at bridge, sort of a cross between Nemesis and the Easter Bunny. I pray to her for help all the time.'

'You're kidding,' I said. 'Why not just ask the clock on the wall?'

'My wife and I prayed every night for children,' Louie offered, 'until we found out that's not how you have them. Now we have seven.'

'Look at this deal from today,' Cy said. 'When dummy turned up with three low diamonds, I needed a miracle to make my contract. So I consulted Brigidda.'

'And she intervened on your behalf?' I asked.

'No, but she gave me some good advice — the same she always gives me. She told me to help myself. Suppose I take the queen of clubs, draw trumps and force out the ace of spades. West knows his side has no more black-suit tricks, so he'll shift to diamonds, and the defense will cash three diamonds.'

'Prayers and supplications won't stop that,' Louie shrugged.

'No, but I did,' Cy said. 'I won the first club with the ace, drew trumps and forced out the ace of spades. Since West was sure East had the queen of clubs, he led another low club so East could win and return a diamond through "my" king. I claimed eleven tricks.'

A winning player is self-reliant. The Turks have a proverb: 'Trust in Allah but tie up your camel.' It's better to help yourself than to trust to fate.

4. September 13

West dealer
N-S vulnerable

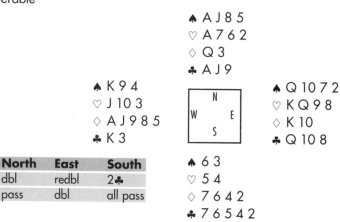

```
                    ♠ A J 8 5
                    ♡ A 7 6 2
                    ◇ Q 3
                    ♣ A J 9
      ♠ K 9 4                      ♠ Q 10 7 2
      ♡ J 10 3         N           ♡ K Q 9 8
      ◇ A J 9 8 5   W     E        ◇ K 10
      ♣ K 3            S           ♣ Q 10 8
                    ♠ 6 3
                    ♡ 5 4
                    ◇ 7 6 4 2
                    ♣ 7 6 5 4 2
```

West	North	East	South
1◇	dbl	redbl	2♣
pass	pass	dbl	all pass

Opening lead: ♡J

'My husband's a podiatrist,' a player at the club told me. 'He often plays in a game with another doctor in his group.'

'Would you say they're arch rivals?' I asked innocently.

'More like arch enemies after this deal. They were partners, defending two clubs doubled. South won the second heart and led a diamond. My husband took the ten and led a third heart.

'South ruffed and lost another diamond. When my husband led a fourth heart, declarer discarded a spade and West threw a diamond. South won my husband's spade shift, ruffed a spade and ruffed a diamond, overruffed. My hubby then led a trump to the king and ace, but his queen won the defenders' last trick.

'South was down only one, and East and West spent the next ten minutes blaming each other.'

The defense had many chances to do better, but I think East was the arch villain: he should lead a trump at Trick 4 since West needs the king for his opening bid. South takes the ace and leads another diamond, but then the defense can clear dummy's trumps and collect a penalty of 800 points.

Bidding Quiz

YOU HOLD: ♠ A J 8 5 ♡ A 7 6 2 ◇ Q 3 ♣ A J 9. Dealer, on your right, opens one diamond. You double, your partner responds one heart and the opening bidder rebids two diamonds. What do you say?

ANSWER: Since the queen of diamonds is surely worth nothing, this is a minimum hand. Your partner may have no points and a weak suit. Pass and let him decide whether to compete. If he has a few values, he won't sell out at the two-level.

Whistfully Yours

South dealer
Both vulnerable

```
                    ♠ 9 8 4
                    ♡ A 10 5
                    ◇ A J 8 7
                    ♣ J 10 9

                    ♠ A Q
                    ♡ K 7 4
                    ◇ Q 10 9 3
                    ♣ A Q 8 7
```

West	North	East	South
			1NT
pass	3NT	all pass	

West leads the six of spades, and you take East's ten with the queen. How do you continue?

Critical Mass

South dealer
N-S vulnerable

```
                    ♠ J 10 6
                    ♡ A 7 4
                    ◇ A J 9 6 4 2
                    ♣ Q

                    ♠ A 9 8
                    ♡ K 6 2
                    ◇ 8 5
                    ♣ A K 10 6 2
```

West	North	East	South
			1♣
pass	1◇	pass	1NT
pass	3NT	all pass	

West leads the queen of hearts. Plan the play.

7. September 25   With a Smile

East dealer
E-W vulnerable

```
              ♠ J 10 6 5 2
              ♡ 9
              ◇ A Q 6 2
              ♣ K 10 6


              ♠ A K Q 8 7 3
              ♡ Q 7 4
              ◇ 5 3
              ♣ 5 3
```

West	North	East	South
		1♡	1♠
pass	2♡	pass	3♠
pass	4♠	all pass	

West leads the deuce of hearts, and East takes the king and shifts to a trump. Plan the play.

8. September 28   Omniscient Play

East dealer
Both vulnerable

```
              ♠ Q 9 6 5 2
              ♡ A Q 6 2
              ◇ K J
              ♣ 5 3


              ♠ A K J 8 3
              ♡ 8 4
              ◇ 8 7 3
              ♣ A 6 4
```

West	North	East	South
		pass	1♠
pass	3♠	pass	4♠
all pass			

West leads the jack of clubs. You take the ace, draw trumps and lead a diamond. When West follows low, do you play the king or the jack?

South dealer
Both vulnerable

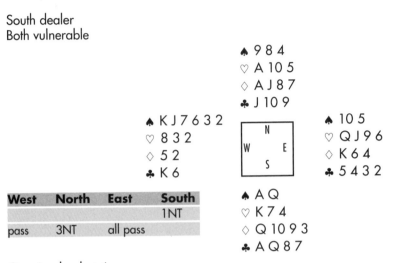

```
                        ♠ 9 8 4
                        ♡ A 10 5
                        ◇ A J 8 7
                        ♣ J 10 9
        ♠ K J 7 6 3 2        ♠ 10 5
        ♡ 8 3 2              ♡ Q J 9 6
        ◇ 5 2          W   E ◇ K 6 4
        ♣ K 6               ♣ 5 4 3 2
                        ♠ A Q
                        ♡ K 7 4
                        ◇ Q 10 9 3
                        ♣ A Q 8 7
```

West	North	East	South
			1NT
pass	3NT	all pass	

Opening lead: ♠6

One denizen of our club — I'll call him Gus — is a crusty whist and poker player who took up bridge to please his wife. Gus is no master of technique, but his card-reading, like that of many whist players, is deadly; and like a good poker player, he can read opponents like a dime novel.

I watched one of our better technicians play this 3NT. He took the queen of spades and led a heart to dummy to finesse in clubs: the idea was to force out West's possible entry before his spades were set up. West won and led another spade, and South took the ace and let the ten of diamonds ride. That finesse also lost, but East had no more spades, and South was home.

At the next table, Gus became declarer at 3NT and slipped by finessing in diamonds at Trick 2. East returned a spade to the ace, and Gus was in trouble: if he finessed in clubs, West would run the spades.

Gus cashed the diamonds, and West, an expert, casually threw the six of clubs and a heart. Gus next took the K-A of hearts and led the jack of clubs from dummy. When East followed low, Gus put up the ace!

'What made you drop the king of clubs?' I asked him.

'The man wouldn't lead a spade with no entry to his suit,' Gus growled. I couldn't argue with success.

Don't rush to criticize West's defense. If he throws a heart and a spade on the diamonds, Gus can take the top hearts and exit with dummy's last spade, forcing West to lead from the king of clubs at the end.

6. September 20   Critical Mass

South dealer
N-S vulnerable

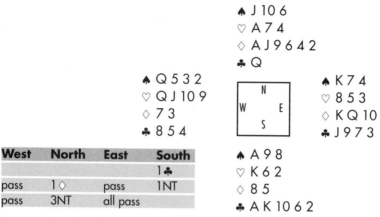

```
               ♠ J 10 6
               ♡ A 7 4
               ◇ A J 9 6 4 2
               ♣ Q
♠ Q 5 3 2                        ♠ K 7 4
♡ Q J 10 9        N              ♡ 8 5 3
◇ 7 3         W       E          ◇ K Q 10
♣ 8 5 4           S             ♣ J 9 7 3
               ♠ A 9 8
               ♡ K 6 2
               ◇ 8 5
               ♣ A K 10 6 2
```

West	North	East	South
			1♣
pass	1◇	pass	1NT
pass	3NT	all pass	

Opening lead: ♡Q

An attractive single woman had joined our club, and Cy the Cynic asked her out for dinner and bridge.

'How'd it go?' I asked.

'Awful,' Cy groaned. 'She didn't like the restaurant and then she harangued my bridge.'

Cy showed me this deal. 'I took the ace of hearts and the queen of clubs and lost a finesse with the jack of spades. I won the next heart, cashed the A-K of clubs and lost a club to the jack. The defenders took two hearts, but I won the diamond shift with the ace and took another spade finesse. I had four clubs, a diamond, two spades and two hearts.'

'Well done,' I said.

'My partner was all over me,' Cy said with a sigh. 'She said I'd make overtricks if I went after her diamonds. But if I take the first heart in my hand to let the eight of diamonds ride, I may go down.'

'And after the game?' I prodded Cy.

'We had a drink at my place,' he said. 'She hated it.'

'She criticized your apartment too?' I said wonderingly.

'I reciprocated,' shrugged Cy. 'I knocked her flat.'

Bidding Quiz

YOU HOLD: ♠ A 9 8 ♡ K 6 2 ◇ 8 5 ♣ A K 10 6 2. Your partner opens one diamond, you respond two clubs and he then bids 3NT. The opponents pass. What do you say?

ANSWER: Your partner should have balanced distribution with slightly too much strength for a 1NT opening. With a minimum balanced hand, his second bid would be 2NT. If you trust him, bid 6NT; if you aren't sure, bid 4NT (quantitative, not ace-asking) to let him decide.

7. September 25 — With a Smile

East dealer
E-W vulnerable

```
                         ♠ J 10 6 5 2
                         ♡ 9
                         ◊ A Q 6 2
                         ♣ K 10 6
         ♠ 4                              ♠ 9
         ♡ J 6 5 2          N             ♡ A K 10 8 3
         ◊ J 9 8        W       E         ◊ K 10 7 4
         ♣ Q 8 7 4 2        S             ♣ A J 9
                         ♠ A K Q 8 7 3
                         ♡ Q 7 4
                         ◊ 5 3
                         ♣ 5 3
```

West	North	East	South
			1♡
		1♥	1♠
pass	2♡	pass	3♠
pass	4♠	all pass	

Opening lead: ♡ 2

'I may be a loser,' Unlucky Louie said ruefully, 'but at least I pay my losses with a smile.'

'Your luck must be improving,' I told him. 'My opponents insist on cash.'

Louie had to pay up after this deal. East took the king of hearts and led a trump. Louie won and finessed with the queen of diamonds, and East took the king and returned a diamond. Louie next ruffed a diamond and tried a club to the king, but East took two clubs to beat the contract.

'Why not try for an endplay?' I asked.

'Won't work,' Louie said. 'I can ruff a heart at Trick 3, return with a trump and ruff a heart; but to get back to my hand again, I must spend dummy's last trump. No endplay.'

Louie must lead a club to the ten at the third trick. East takes the jack and leads the ace of hearts. Louie ruffs in dummy, returns a trump to his hand, throws a club from dummy on the queen of hearts and leads a club. East must return a diamond to dummy's A-Q or concede a ruff-sluff.

Bidding Quiz

YOU HOLD: ♠ 9 ♡ A K 10 8 3 ◊ K 10 7 4 ♣ A J 9. Your partner opens one diamond, and the next player passes. What do you say?

ANSWER: If partner has a suitable minimum opening bid with five good diamonds, the ace of spades and the queen of hearts, he'll have a good chance for thirteen tricks in diamonds. Hence it must be best to show your interest in slam immediately. Jump to two hearts, intending to support diamonds at your next turn.

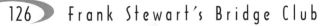

8. September 28 — Omniscient Play

East dealer
Both vulnerable

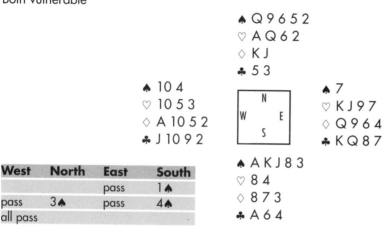

♠ Q 9 6 5 2
♡ A Q 6 2
♢ K J
♣ 5 3

♠ 10 4
♡ 10 5 3
♢ A 10 5 2
♣ J 10 9 2

♠ 7
♡ K J 9 7
♢ Q 9 6 4
♣ K Q 8 7

♠ A K J 8 3
♡ 8 4
♢ 8 7 3
♣ A 6 4

West	North	East	South
		pass	1♠
pass	3♠	pass	4♠
all pass			

Opening lead: ♣ J

'My partner in this deal was a complete know-it-all,' Cy the Cynic grumbled to me, 'and people who think they know everything really annoy those of us who actually do.'

Cy took the ace of clubs, drew trumps, led a diamond toward dummy and guessed to play the jack. East took the queen, cashed a club and led a diamond to West's ace. When the heart finesse lost, Cy went down.

'North said I should guess right in diamonds,' Cy said. 'He said East hadn't opened the bidding and was marked with the K-Q of clubs, so I couldn't lose by playing the king of diamonds. If East had the ace, he couldn't also have the king of hearts, and I'd lose two diamonds and one club.'

'A second-degree assumption', I remarked. 'You make an assumption about the location of one honor and see where it leads.'

'But how do I know East has the K-Q of clubs?' Cy demanded. 'If West led the jack from K-J-10, I might as well read tea leaves to place the missing red-suit honors. Of course, that possibility never occurred to my omniscient partner.'

Cy had a point, but he should go right in diamonds anyway. For West to lead from the K-J-10 of clubs would be unattractive — unless he had a diamond holding from which he was also reluctant to lead. If West's diamonds were Q-10-5-2 or 10-6-5-2, he'd probably prefer leading a diamond to leading from the K-J-10 of clubs; but West might risk a club lead rather than bang down the ace of diamonds. So South should put up the king on the first diamond.

9. October 1   Don't Be a Hypocrite

North dealer
N-S vulnerable

```
              ♠ A J 7 2
              ♡ 6
              ◇ A 9 8 3
              ♣ A 7 6 3

              ♠ 8
              ♡ K Q J 5 4 2
              ◇ K 5 4
              ♣ K 4 2
```

West	North	East	South
	1◇	pass	1♡
pass	1♠	pass	4♡
all pass			

West leads the jack of clubs. Plan the play.

10. October 4   Footing the Bill

South dealer
Both vulnerable

```
              ♠ A Q 10 7 2
              ♡ 8 6 3
              ◇ A J 10
              ♣ Q 7

              ♠ K J 9 8 4
              ♡ A Q 7
              ◇ 8 5 4
              ♣ A 6
```

West	North	East	South
			1♠
pass	3♠	pass	4♠
all pass			

West leads the deuce of hearts, and East puts up the king. Plan the play.

11. October 8 — Bring, Brang, Brung?

North dealer
Neither vulnerable

```
              ♠ Q 8
              ♡ A Q 10 7 4
              ◇ A Q 7 3
              ♣ J 6

              ♠ K J 10 9 5 2
              ♡ —
              ◇ 5
              ♣ A K 10 8 7 3
```

West	North	East	South
	1♡	pass	1♠
pass	2◇	pass	3♣
pass	3♠	pass	6♠
all pass			

West leads the ten of diamonds. Plan the play.

12. October 10 — Better by Halves

South dealer
E-W vulnerable

```
              ♠ Q 7 6 5 3
              ♡ K 9
              ◇ K 4 2
              ♣ A 7 6

              ♠ 2
              ♡ A Q 10 8 6 4
              ◇ A 9 5
              ♣ J 3 2
```

West	North	East	South
			1♡
pass	1♠	pass	2♡
pass	2NT	pass	3♡
pass	4♡ (!)	all pass	

West leads the queen of diamonds. Plan the play.

9. October 1

North dealer
N-S vulnerable

```
                        ♠ A J 7 2
                        ♡ 6
                        ♢ A 9 8 3
                        ♣ A 7 6 3
    ♠ Q 10 5                              ♠ K 9 6 4 3
    ♡ A 10              N                 ♡ 9 8 7 3
    ♢ Q 10 7 2      W       E             ♢ J 6
    ♣ J 10 9 8          S                 ♣ Q 5
                        ♠ 8
                        ♡ K Q J 5 4 2
                        ♢ K 5 4
                        ♣ K 4 2
```

West	North	East	South
	1◇	pass	1♡
pass	1♠	pass	4♡
all pass			

Opening lead: ♣ J

'My partner's a hypocrite,' a pupil complained to me at the club.

'She claims there's too much sex and violence on her VCR?' I asked.

'No, she tells me to do something, then fusses at me when I do it. She always wants me to draw trumps promptly, but in this deal she said I should wait.'

South took the ace of clubs and led a trump to her king. West won and led another club, and South won and cashed the Q-J of trumps. West showed out, and South lost another trump, a club and a diamond.

'It can't matter when I draw trumps,' South told me. 'I have four certain losers.'

South must win the first club with the king, take the ace of spades, ruff a spade and lead the king of trumps. West wins and leads another club, and South takes the ace, ruffs a spade and cashes the Q-J of trumps.

When West discards, South cashes the top diamonds and ruffs dummy's last spade for her tenth trick. The defense wins the last two tricks — with West's high cards and with East's winning trump! (South might also succeed with a minor-suit squeeze against West.)

Bidding Quiz

YOU HOLD: ♠ K 9 6 4 3 ♡ 9 8 7 3 ◇ J 6 ♣ Q 5. Dealer, on your left, opens one heart. Your partner doubles, and the next player raises to two hearts. What do you say?

ANSWER: Bid two spades. To pass would betray timidity. Your partner promises opening values or more, good spade support and shortness in hearts, and the play in a spade contract should go beautifully. In fact, if partner raises to three spades, you'll bid four spades.

10. October 4

Footing the Bill

South dealer
Both vulnerable

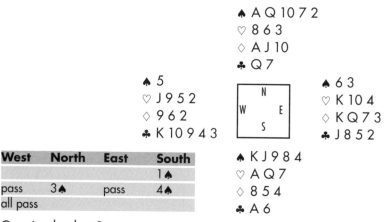

```
                    ♠ A Q 10 7 2
                    ♡ 8 6 3
                    ◇ A J 10
                    ♣ Q 7
  ♠ 5                              ♠ 6 3
  ♡ J 9 5 2          N             ♡ K 10 4
  ◇ 9 6 2        W       E         ◇ K Q 7 3
  ♣ K 10 9 4 3       S             ♣ J 8 5 2
                    ♠ K J 9 8 4
                    ♡ A Q 7
                    ◇ 8 5 4
                    ♣ A 6
```

West	North	East	South
			1♠
pass	3♠	pass	4♠
all pass			

Opening lead: ♡2

'Can you define 'pedestrian'?' a player at the club asked me.

'Someone who thought the tank still had gas in it when the needle read empty?' I offered.

'I went down in this deal,' he said, 'and my partner said the play was pedestrian. Why?'

South captured East's king on the first heart, drew trumps and led a diamond to dummy's ten. East took the queen and returned a heart, and South won and tried another diamond finesse with the jack. East produced the king and shifted accurately to a club, and South had to lose a club to West's king and a heart to his jack. Down one.

South was cold for four spades on an endplay, but I wouldn't call the play pedestrian: South must refuse the first heart! He wins the next heart, draws trumps, cashes the other high heart and leads the ace and a low club.

The defense is sunk. West takes the king and leads a diamond; but when East wins, he must lead a club, giving South a ruff-sluff, or return a diamond to dummy's tenace.

Bidding Quiz

YOU HOLD: ♠ 6 3 ♡ K 10 4 ◇ K Q 7 3 ♣ J 8 5 2. Your partner opens one spade, you respond 1NT, he bids two diamonds and you raise to three diamonds. Partner next bids three hearts. What do you say?

ANSWER: Partner's three hearts suggests game and portrays a hand with shortness in clubs: his pattern may be 5-3-5-0 or 5-3-4-1. (He doesn't have four hearts since he didn't bid two hearts over your 1NT.) Since most of your values look useful, bid five diamonds.

11. October 8

Bring, Brang, Brung?

North dealer
Neither vulnerable

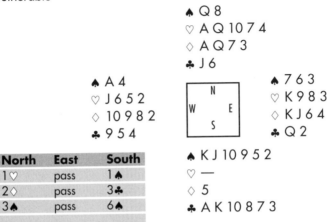

```
                    ♠ Q 8
                    ♡ A Q 10 7 4
                    ◇ A Q 7 3
                    ♣ J 6
    ♠ A 4                          ♠ 7 6 3
    ♡ J 6 5 2            N         ♡ K 9 8 3
    ◇ 10 9 8 2      W       E      ◇ K J 6 4
    ♣ 9 5 4             S          ♣ Q 2
                    ♠ K J 10 9 5 2
                    ♡ —
                    ◇ 5
                    ♣ A K 10 8 7 3
```

West	North	East	South
	1♡	pass	1♠
pass	2◇	pass	3♣
pass	3♠	pass	6♠
all pass			

Opening lead: ◇ 10

My old friend the English professor left his university teaching position and retired, part-time, to his farm. (His car now bears a bumper sticker that enjoins, 'Split wood, not infinitives.') Still, he finds time to visit the bridge club.

In this deal, the professor, North, put down his dummy just as the club waiter asked if he wanted his glass refilled.

'Ibid, ibid!' the prof nodded gently, but then watched in agitation as South proceeded to mangle a slam.

South took the ace of diamonds and correctly cashed the A-K of clubs. When the queen fell, South thought he could afford to start the trumps; but West won the second trump and led another club, and East ruffed to defeat the contract.

'I couldn't have brung that one home,' South drawled, and the prof shuddered. 'It's bring, brought, brought,' he said tersely. 'Moreover, six spades was cold. All you must do is ruff a third club in dummy before you lead a trump. Then the ace of trumps is your only loser.'

Bidding Quiz

YOU HOLD: ♠ Q 8 ♡ A Q 10 7 4 ◇ A Q 7 3 ♣ J 6. Your partner opens one spade, you respond two hearts and he rebids three clubs. The opponents pass. What do you say?

ANSWER: Partner's second bid at the three-level promises extra strength; with minimum values, he'd rebid two spades or perhaps 2NT. Bid three diamonds. If partner next bids 3NT, you'll raise to 4NT to invite slam in notrump. If he bids three hearts, you can try six hearts.

12. October 10

South dealer
E-W vulnerable

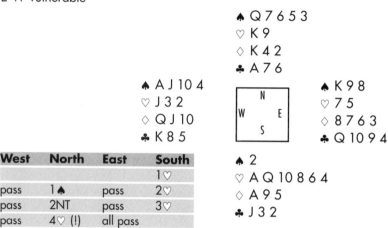

	♠ Q 7 6 5 3	
	♡ K 9	
	◇ K 4 2	
	♣ A 7 6	
♠ A J 10 4		♠ K 9 8
♡ J 3 2	N	♡ 7 5
◇ Q J 10	W E	◇ 8 7 6 3
♣ K 8 5	S	♣ Q 10 9 4
	♠ 2	
	♡ A Q 10 8 6 4	
	◇ A 9 5	
	♣ J 3 2	

West	North	East	South
			1♡
pass	1♠	pass	2♡
pass	2NT	pass	3♡
pass	4♡ (!)	all pass	

Opening lead: ◇Q

'Cy the Cynic was spouting off yesterday,' Unlucky Louie told me. 'He said half the players in our club know nothing about bidding and the other half know nothing about play.'

'What an allegation!' I groaned.

'Especially since exactly the reverse is true,' agreed Louie.

Louie, South, took the ace of diamonds and ran five rounds of trumps. East-West discarded well, and Louie lost two clubs, a spade and a diamond. Down one.

'My partner had no business bidding four hearts,' Louie grumbled. 'He could have bid 3NT — an icy contract — at his second turn; but once he bid 2NT, which limited his strength, he should have passed my signoff at three hearts.'

North may have been in one half of our members, but Louie belonged in the other half. At Trick 2 Louie must concede a spade. He wins the diamond return in dummy, ruffs a spade, risks a trump to the nine(!) and ruffs a spade.

Louie can then return to dummy with a trump to the king, ruff a spade, draw trumps and go to the ace of clubs to cash the good spade for his tenth trick.

Bidding Quiz

YOU HOLD: ♠ Q 7 6 5 3 ♡ K 9 ◇ K 4 2 ♣ A 7 6. Your partner opens one diamond, you bid one spade and he then jumps to 2NT. The opponents pass. What do you say?

ANSWER: Partner has a balanced 19 or 20 points, and your hand is worth 13 points. Since slam is possible, raise to 4NT, asking him to go on with a maximum. If he stops off to bid five diamonds next, you'll bid six diamonds; that'll be best if he holds ♠ K 4 ♡ A Q 3 ◇ A Q J 9 6 ♣ K 4 3.

13. October 15 — Trump Loser

West dealer
Both vulnerable

```
            ♠ 8 5
            ♡ J 10 7
            ◇ J 8 2
            ♣ A K 8 5 2

            ♠ A K Q J 7 6 4 2
            ♡ A K 6
            ◇ A 3
            ♣ —
```

West	North	East	South
pass	pass	3◇	6♠
all pass			

West leads the four of diamonds. Plan the play.

14. October 18 — Encore, Encore!

South dealer
Both vulnerable

```
            ♠ Q 10 8 5 2
            ♡ K 10 9 8
            ◇ 8 5
            ♣ 7 3

            ♠ 7
            ♡ A Q 7 4 2
            ◇ A 7 4
            ♣ A K 6 4
```

West	North	East	South
			1♡
dbl	3♡	pass	4♡
all pass			

West leads the king of spades and shifts to a trump. Dummy's eight wins. Both defenders follow to the A-K of clubs. How do you continue?

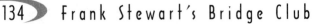

15. October 21 — Hair-Raising Deal

West dealer
Both vulnerable

```
              ♠ 4 2
              ♡ J 10 5 3
              ◇ A Q 6
              ♣ A Q 6 2

              ♠ K J 7 6 5 3
              ♡ 7
              ◇ K 9 8 4
              ♣ K 5
```

West	North	East	South
1♡	pass	pass	1♠
pass	2NT	pass	4♠
all pass			

West leads the king of hearts and continues with the ace. Plan the play.

16. October 23 — Fortuitous Play

East dealer
Neither vulnerable

```
              ♠ A K 9 7 2
              ♡ J 7 6 3
              ◇ A 7 2
              ♣ Q

              ♠ Q 6 4
              ♡ A K 9 8 4
              ◇ 9 4 3
              ♣ A 7
```

West	North	East	South
		3♣	3♡
pass	4♣	pass	4♡
pass	6♡	all pass	

West leads the queen of diamonds. You take the ace and cash the A-K of trumps, and East discards. How do you continue?

13. October 15

West dealer
Both vulnerable

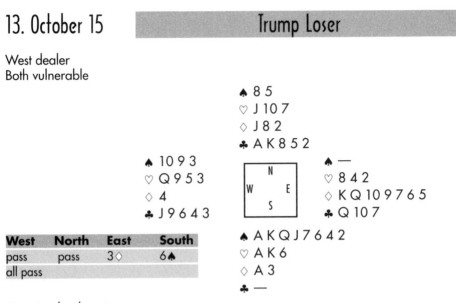

```
                    ♠ 8 5
                    ♡ J 10 7
                    ◇ J 8 2
                    ♣ A K 8 5 2
    ♠ 10 9 3                         ♠ —
    ♡ Q 9 5 3            N           ♡ 8 4 2
    ◇ 4            W           E      ◇ K Q 10 9 7 6 5
    ♣ J 9 6 4 3          S          ♣ Q 10 7
                    ♠ A K Q J 7 6 4 2
                    ♡ A K 6
                    ◇ A 3
                    ♣ —
```

West	North	East	South
pass	pass	3◇	6♠
all pass			

Opening lead: ◇ 4

'Hey,' said a voice on my phone, 'didja hear Ed lost a trump trick with eight of 'em to the A-K-Q-J?'

Ed is one of the club's best players; I couldn't believe he'd contrived a trump loser with that holding.

'Did he get a 5-0 break?' I asked.

'Trumps broke 3-0,' laughed my caller.

'Let's hear what happened,' I said.

It seemed Ed had picked up the massive South hand and had chosen a time-saving leap to slam over East's preempt. West led a diamond, and Ed took the ace and counted thirteen tricks — two of which looked out of reach.

Some players would have raced off the trumps, hoping for a defensive slip. An alert West would throw his clubs and would get two hearts in the end.

'Ed couldn't get to dummy on his own,' my caller said, 'so he got his opponent to help. Ed cashed the A-K of trumps. West did his best by dropping the nine and ten, but Ed threw him in by leading the deuce of trumps. West then had to lead a club or a heart, and Ed was home.'

Bidding Quiz

YOU HOLD: ♠ — ♡ 8 4 2 ◇ K Q 10 9 7 6 5 ♣ Q 10 7. You open three diamonds, the next player bids three spades, your partner bids 3NT and the player on your right tries four spades. What do you say?

ANSWER: It's not clear what's going on: your partner may have a good hand or may have bid 3NT as a pure bluff. In any case, your preempt described your hand, more or less; he knows more about your hand than you do about his. Pass.

14. October 18

South dealer
Both vulnerable

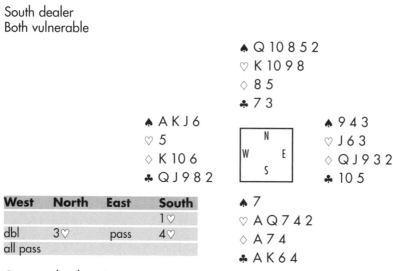

♠ Q 10 8 5 2
♡ K 10 9 8
♢ 8 5
♣ 7 3

♠ A K J 6
♡ 5
♢ K 10 6
♣ Q J 9 8 2

N
W E
S

♠ 9 4 3
♡ J 6 3
♢ Q J 9 3 2
♣ 10 5

♠ 7
♡ A Q 7 4 2
♢ A 7 4
♣ A K 6 4

West	North	East	South
			1♡
dbl	3♡	pass	4♡
all pass			

Opening lead: ♠K

The bridge club smiled when Unlucky Louie told us his wife is expecting — again — at 41. Perhaps inspired, Louie gave a fine performance in a team game that day. Against four hearts (bid at both tables), West cashed a spade and shifted to a trump. Dummy's eight won, and both Souths then took the A-K of clubs and led a third club.

At one table South ruffed with the nine, and East overruffed with the jack and led his last trump. South could then ruff only one loser in dummy and took only nine tricks.

Louie did better. Instead of ruffing the third club, he threw a diamond from dummy: a loser on a loser. East did his best by ruffing West's trick to lead another trump, but Louie still got two ruffs in dummy, five trumps in his hand, two clubs and a diamond.

'Encore, encore,' a kibitzer said approvingly.

'If it's a girl,' Louie said, 'that'll be her middle name. "Encore". '

'How come?'

'She wasn't on the program at all,' Louie replied sheepishly.

Bidding Quiz

YOU HOLD: ♠ A K J 6 ♡ 5 ♢ K 10 6 ♣ Q J 9 8 2. You open one club, your partner responds one heart, you bid one spade and he rebids two hearts. The opponents pass. What do you say?

ANSWER: Partners always seem to rebid suits you don't like, but a misfit is no reason to keep bidding. Partner has a weak hand with long hearts, and his hand may take no tricks unless hearts are trumps. Pass and hope he wins eight tricks. Another bid risks a minus score.

15. October 21 — Hair-Raising Deal

West dealer
Both vulnerable

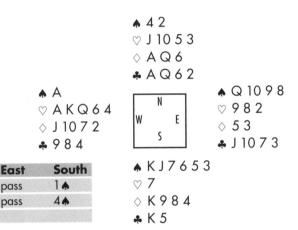

```
              ♠ 4 2
              ♡ J 10 5 3
              ◊ A Q 6
              ♣ A Q 6 2
♠ A                        ♠ Q 10 9 8
♡ A K Q 6 4      N         ♡ 9 8 2
◊ J 10 7 2    W     E      ◊ 5 3
♣ 9 8 4          S         ♣ J 10 7 3
              ♠ K J 7 6 5 3
              ♡ 7
              ◊ K 9 8 4
              ♣ K 5
```

West	North	East	South
1♡	pass	pass	1♠
pass	2NT	pass	4♠
all pass			

Opening lead: ♡K

Unlucky Louie showed up at the club looking like his hair had tangled with an angry string trimmer.

'We're trying to cut expenses,' Louie announced, 'and my wife bought me a do-it-your-self haircut kit. It paid for itself right away.'

'You saved $12 at the barber shop?' I said, unimpressed.

'And my wife cancelled all our dinner reservations for the next three weeks,' said Louie.

Louie had a hair-raising experience in this deal. He ruffed the second heart, led a club to dummy and returned a trump. East played the ten. Louie had the jack out of his hand and on its way to the table when he paused. West was marked with the ace of spades for his opening bid, and if East had the queen, a finesse would work just as well later. So Louie replaced his jack with the three.

When West had to take the ace, Louie was safe by a hair. He took the diamond return in dummy, led a trump to the jack, cashed the king, and claimed his game, losing one more trump.

Bidding Quiz

YOU HOLD: ♠ A ♡ A K Q 6 4 ◊ J 10 7 2 ♣ 9 8 4. You open one heart, and your partner bids one spade. The opponents pass. What do you say?

ANSWER: Bid two diamonds. Since the five-card heart suit is strong, some out-of-date textbooks would recommend a rebid of two hearts; but if partner has a weak hand with support for diamonds and none for hearts, you'll be glad you mentioned your second suit. If partner next bids two spades, you'll pass, of course.

16. October 23

East dealer
Neither vulnerable

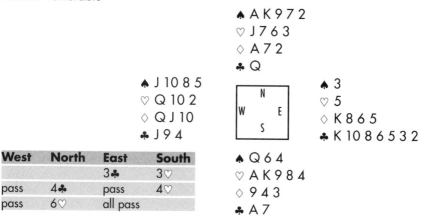

```
              ♠ A K 9 7 2
              ♡ J 7 6 3
              ◊ A 7 2
              ♣ Q
  ♠ J 10 8 5              ♠ 3
  ♡ Q 10 2        N       ♡ 5
  ◊ Q J 10    W       E   ◊ K 8 6 5
  ♣ J 9 4         S       ♣ K 10 8 6 5 3 2
              ♠ Q 6 4
              ♡ A K 9 8 4
              ◊ 9 4 3
              ♣ A 7
```

West	North	East	South
		3♣	3♡
pass	4♣	pass	4♡
pass	6♡	all pass	

Opening lead: ◊Q

My friend the English professor is a stickler for word usage. He once chastised me for writing that a contract 'foundered and sank.'

' "Founder" has a built-in sink,' he told me. 'That's what the word means.'

The prof, West, decided South was ready for a club opening lead and tried the queen of diamonds. South took the ace, cashed the A-K of trumps, shrugged, and led the queen of spades and another spade. The prof played low, and declarer played the nine from dummy! He took the A-K of spades and the fifth spade, throwing his remaining diamonds, and lost only one trump trick.

'That was fortuitous in spades,' growled East.

'The word is "fortunate", ' said the prof. ' "Fortuitous" means "happening by chance", and declarer knew exactly what he was doing. He had to pitch two diamonds before I ruffed; hence he had to assume I held four spades.'

The prof was right on both counts. South might have cost himself an extra undertrick but took his only chance for the slam.

Bidding Quiz

YOU HOLD: ♠ Q 6 4 ♡ A K 9 8 4 ◊ 9 4 3 ♣ A 7. You open one heart, your partner responds two diamonds, you rebid two hearts and he next bids two spades. The opponents pass. What do you say?

ANSWER: Bid three diamonds. Since you have prime values and only a single club 'stopper', it would be questionable to bid notrump. Showing support for partner when you can is a basic bidding principle. If 3NT is your best contract, you'll still have time to get there.

17. October 26 — Grapefruit Mellows?

East dealer
E-W vulnerable

```
              ♠ K 10 5 4
              ♡ A J 6 4
              ◇ 8 3
              ♣ K 6 3
        ┌─────────────┐        ♠ 9
        │      N      │        ♡ K 10 8 7 3
        │ W         E │        ◇ J 6 5
        │      S      │        ♣ J 8 4 2
        └─────────────┘
```

West	North	East	South
		pass	1♠
pass	3♠	pass	4♠
all pass			

West leads the deuce of trumps. Declarer wins in dummy and leads the three of diamonds: five, king, ace. West continues with the ace and another trump, and you pitch a heart and a club. South wins the third trump in dummy and leads the eight of diamonds. Do you play the six or the jack?

18. October 28 — Marked Cards?

South dealer
Both vulnerable

```
              ♠ K 5 4
              ♡ K J 7 5 2
              ◇ 9 6 2
              ♣ A 9



              ♠ A 8 2
              ♡ A 3
              ◇ A K Q 5 3
              ♣ J 7 4
```

West	North	East	South
			1◇
pass	1♡	pass	2NT
pass	3NT	all pass	

West leads the king of clubs. Plan the play.

I hope you enjoy **Frank Stewart's Bridge Club**. Thanks for your order. The proceeds from my sales of this book will go to charities in my town. Other books of mine also available from me:

Becoming an Expert. A big treasury of tips to move your game to the next level. $19.95

A Christmas Stocking. Six short stories about events at my imaginary bridge club during the Holiday season. Hardbound and illustrated. $10.95

The Bidder's Bible. Focuses on judgment. Improves your bidding by showing where experts went wrong. $16.95

My Bridge and Yours. Compare your decisions with mine in 70 deals. $11.95

Two-Minute Bridge Tips. The best of "Daily Bridge Club". $11.95

Postpaid, autographed on request. PO Box 962, Fayette AL 35555.

19. October 30   Tolerance for Error

North dealer
Both vulnerable

```
              ♠ K Q 2
              ♡ 7 6 3
              ◇ A J 10 7 4
              ♣ A 9

              ♠ A J 10 9 8 7
              ♡ A 8 5
              ◇ 6 3
              ♣ 5 4
```

West	North	East	South
	1◇	pass	1♠
pass	2♠	pass	4♠
all pass			

West leads the king of clubs. Plan the play.

20. November 3   Artistic Play

South dealer
N-S vulnerable

```
              ♠ Q J 10 7
              ♡ 10 7 6 3
              ◇ Q
              ♣ A 7 5 3

              ♠ A
              ♡ A 5
              ◇ A 10 7 6 4 2
              ♣ K Q J 2
```

West	North	East	South
			1◇
pass	1♡	pass	2♣
pass	3♣	pass	3◇
pass	3♠	pass	3NT
all pass			

West leads the four of hearts: three, nine ... Plan the play.

17. October 26 — Grapefruit Mellows?

East dealer
E-W vulnerable

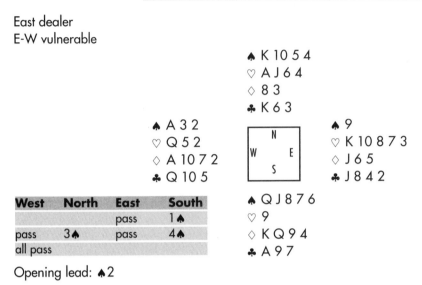

```
                    ♠ K 10 5 4
                    ♡ A J 6 4
                    ◇ 8 3
                    ♣ K 6 3
   ♠ A 3 2                          ♠ 9
   ♡ Q 5 2           N              ♡ K 10 8 7 3
   ◇ A 10 7 2     W     E           ◇ J 6 5
   ♣ Q 10 5          S              ♣ J 8 4 2
                    ♠ Q J 8 7 6
                    ♡ 9
                    ◇ K Q 9 4
                    ♣ A 9 7
```

West	North	East	South
		pass	1♠
pass	3♠	pass	4♠
all pass			

Opening lead: ♠2

'For a minute I thought Grapefruit had mellowed,' a club player told me. He meant our member with the acid disposition.

'He was playing rubber bridge,' my friend said, 'and cut someone's out-of-town guest as his partner. Grapefruit led a trump against four spades, and South won in dummy and led a diamond to his king. Grapefruit took the ace and led the ace and a low trump.'

'Good defense,' I said. 'South couldn't ruff two diamonds in dummy.'

'South next led dummy's eight of diamonds,' my friend went on. 'East played low, and South let the eight ride to Grapefruit's ten. South later took the Q-9 of diamonds, threw a club from dummy and ruffed a club to make his game. If East covers the eight of diamonds — and he should — South goes down.'

'What did Grapefruit say?' I asked.

'He said, "Never mind, you did your best". '

'No wonder you thought Grapefruit had mellowed,' I remarked.

'He wasn't finished. He added, "But whoever let you in here should be shot". '

Bidding Quiz

YOU HOLD: ♠ Q J 8 7 6 ♡ 9 ◇ K Q 9 4 ♣ A 9 7. You open one spade, your partner responds two hearts, you rebid two spades and he rebids three hearts. The opponents pass. What do you say?

ANSWER: Pass. Partner has six or seven hearts but no more than 11 points. With a better hand, he could have jumped to four hearts or temporized by bidding a new suit. Since you have skinny values and no heart fit, quit here. Don't even think of bidding 3NT.

18. October 28

South dealer
Both vulnerable

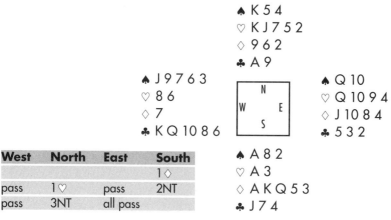

```
                    ♠ K 5 4
                    ♡ K J 7 5 2
                    ◊ 9 6 2
                    ♣ A 9
   ♠ J 9 7 6 3              N        ♠ Q 10
   ♡ 8 6              W           E  ♡ Q 10 9 4
   ◊ 7                    S        ◊ J 10 8 4
   ♣ K Q 10 8 6                      ♣ 5 3 2
                    ♠ A 8 2
                    ♡ A 3
                    ◊ A K Q 5 3
                    ♣ J 7 4
```

West	North	East	South
			1◊
pass	1♡	pass	2NT
pass	3NT	all pass	

Opening lead: ♣K

I was sitting in the club lounge with Cy the Cynic when a worried-looking player came up.

'What do you do,' he asked, 'if you think someone is cheating?'

'I'd place a heavy bet on him,' Cy replied, in character.

'What happened?' I frowned.

'I was West, and South took the ace of clubs and led the nine of diamonds from dummy. He said he intended to let it ride if my partner played low. When partner covered with the ten, South won, went back to dummy and led the six of diamonds. East played low — to cover wouldn't help him — and South played low! He took ten tricks.

'I don't know how South knew East had all the diamonds. Maybe he broke in here last night and marked the cards.'

'I think not,' I said. 'His play was correct.'

South needs only four diamond tricks to make game and is in danger only if East gets in to return a club. If West has the singleton four of diamonds, South is helpless, but South's play catered to any other singleton with West. (Yes, South could also make 3NT by endplaying West.)

Bidding Quiz

YOU HOLD: ♠ J 9 7 6 3 ♡ 8 6 ◊ 7 ♣ K Q 10 8 6. Your partner opens one diamond, you respond one spade and he rebids two diamonds. The opponents pass. What do you say?

ANSWER: Unless you just received a large inheritance, pass. Partner has minimum values with six or more diamonds, and you're going nowhere. You might do better in clubs, but if you bid three clubs, a forcing bid in a new suit, you'd promise more strength. Don't fight a misfit.

19. October 30

North dealer
Both vulnerable

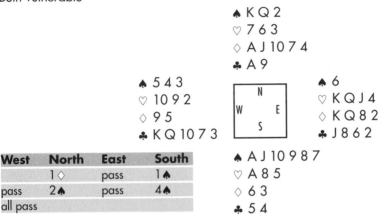

```
                    ♠ K Q 2
                    ♡ 7 6 3
                    ◇ A J 10 7 4
                    ♣ A 9
     ♠ 5 4 3              N           ♠ 6
     ♡ 10 9 2        W        E       ♡ K Q J 4
     ◇ 9 5               S           ◇ K Q 8 2
     ♣ K Q 10 7 3                    ♣ J 8 6 2
                    ♠ A J 10 9 8 7
                    ♡ A 8 5
                    ◇ 6 3
                    ♣ 5 4
```

West	North	East	South
	1◇	pass	1♠
pass	2♠	pass	4♠
all pass			

Opening lead: ♣K

I was in the lounge when Dr. Ed Fitch, our club president, straggled in from a club Board meeting.

'Three people want Grapefruit dismembered,' Ed sighed, meaning our player with an acid tongue.

'They want him expelled from the club?'

'They want him torn limb from limb. Grapefruit was North, and South won the first club, drew trumps and lost a diamond finesse with the ten. East cashed a club and shifted to hearts. South won and tried a diamond to the jack. Two down.

'We ought to call the man "Grape-nuts",' Ed went on, 'since that's what he went. South got up and left in disgust, and Grapefruit told him not to bray on his way out.'

'South's play wasn't bad,' I said, 'but he had a better play: he could lead a low diamond from dummy at the second trick. East wins and cashes a club, but South wins the heart shift and continues with ace of diamonds, diamond ruff, queen of trumps, diamond ruff, ace and king of trumps. The last diamond is good.'

Ed nodded, no doubt wishing Grapefruit were more tolerant of his partners' errors.

Bidding Quiz

YOU HOLD: ♠ K Q 2 ♡ 7 6 3 ◇ A J 10 7 4 ♣ A 9. You open one diamond, your partner responds one heart, you bid 1NT and he bids two spades. The opponents pass. What do you say?

ANSWER: Partner promises longer hearts than spades; hence return to three hearts. With stronger hearts, you'd jump to four hearts. Since your 1NT denied a four-card spade suit, to raise to three spades wouldn't be a terrible action, but you shouldn't persist with notrump.

South dealer
N-S vulnerable

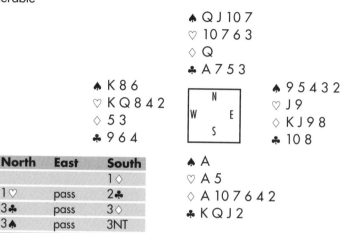

♠ Q J 10 7
♡ 10 7 6 3
◇ Q
♣ A 7 5 3

♠ K 8 6
♡ K Q 8 4 2
◇ 5 3
♣ 9 6 4

♠ 9 5 4 3 2
♡ J 9
◇ K J 9 8
♣ 10 8

♠ A
♡ A 5
◇ A 10 7 6 4 2
♣ K Q J 2

West	North	East	South
			1◇
pass	1♡	pass	2♣
pass	3♣	pass	3◇
pass	3♠	pass	3NT
all pass			

Opening lead: ♡4

'Somebody told me you used to manage an art gallery,' I mentioned to Cy the Cynic, whose background is something of a mystery at the bridge club.

'Only for a few months,' Cy replied blandly. 'I never got the hang of it.'

I groaned.

'Besides,' Cy went on, 'I felt some of our paintings were hung only because the artist wasn't available.'

Cy handled the play of this deal like Van Gogh. When East played the nine on the first heart, Cy took the ace. Cy knew he was in danger only if West had five hearts, but then if East's last heart was an honor, Cy could block the suit by winning immediately.

Cy next cashed the ace of spades and the K-Q of clubs. When both defenders followed, Cy overtook the jack of clubs with the ace and led the queen of spades to force out the king.

West led another low heart to East's jack; but Cy won the diamond return, got to dummy by leading the deuce of clubs to the seven and took the J-10 of spades to make the contract.

Bidding Quiz

YOU HOLD: ♠ Q J 10 7 ♡ 10 7 6 3 ◇ Q ♣ A 7 5 3. Your partner opens one diamond, you respond one heart and he then bids 1NT. The opponents pass. What do you say?

ANSWER: Your partner promises 13 to 15 points with balanced distribution (but not with four cards in spades since then he'd have bid one spade at his second turn). Game is out of the question, and as far as you can tell, 1NT will be as good a partscore as any. Pass.

21. November 6   Drama in the Deal

North dealer
N-S vulnerable

```
              ♠ A 3
              ♡ 10 6 2
              ◇ K 5 3
              ♣ A K 8 7 4

              ♠ J 6
              ♡ A K Q J 7 4
              ◇ A J
              ♣ J 6 2
```

West	North	East	South
	1♣	pass	1♡
2♠	3♡	pass	4NT
pass	5♡	pass	6♡
all pass			

West leads the king of spades. Plan the play.

22. November 9   Exact Hindsight

North dealer
Both vulnerable

```
              ♠ Q J 10
              ♡ A J 9 6
              ◇ A K 7
              ♣ J 10 9

              ♠ A 9 8 7 6
              ♡ K 3 2
              ◇ 4
              ♣ A K 6 4
```

West	North	East	South
	1NT	pass	3♠
pass	4♠	pass	6♠
all pass			

West leads the queen of diamonds. Plan the play.

23. November 11 — Procrastination Pays

South dealer
Both vulnerable

```
              ♠ 10 6 3
              ♡ 8 2
              ◇ Q 6 5 4 3 2
              ♣ A J

              ♠ J 2
              ♡ A K J 6 3
              ◇ A K J 10
              ♣ 10 6
```

West	North	East	South
			1♡
pass	1NT	pass	2◇
pass	3◇	pass	5◇
all pass			

West leads the nine of diamonds. Plan the play.

24. November 14 — Patience Needed: Now!

North dealer
Both vulnerable

```
              ♠ 9 5
              ♡ 10 6 4 2
              ◇ A K 9 8
              ♣ K Q 10

              ♠ A 8 4 2
              ♡ A 7 5 3
              ◇ 7 4
              ♣ A J 3
```

West	North	East	South
	1◇	pass	1♡
pass	2♡	pass	3NT
pass	4♡	all pass	

West leads the three of spades. Plan the play.

21. November 6

North dealer
N-S vulnerable

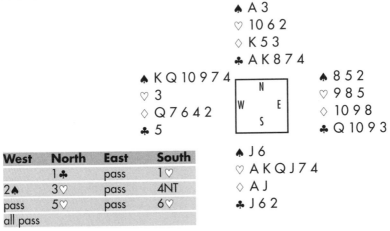

	♠ A 3	
	♡ 10 6 2	
	◇ K 5 3	
	♣ A K 8 7 4	

♠ K Q 10 9 7 4   ♠ 8 5 2
♡ 3   ♡ 9 8 5
◇ Q 7 6 4 2   ◇ 10 9 8
♣ 5   ♣ Q 10 9 3

♠ J 6
♡ A K Q J 7 4
◇ A J
♣ J 6 2

West	North	East	South
	1♣	pass	1♡
2♠	3♡	pass	4NT
pass	5♡	pass	6♡
all pass			

Opening lead: ♠K

My friend the English professor said this deal reminded him of Shakespeare: the bidding was a comedy and the play was a tragedy.

'South might have jumped to two hearts,' the prof told me, 'and his ace-asking 4NT was silly: if North showed one ace, South wouldn't know what to do. But much ado about nothing: North had two aces, and South tried six hearts.'

South took the ace of spades, drew trumps and cashed the A-K of clubs. When West discarded, South couldn't even gain by trying a finesse with the jack of diamonds for his twelfth trick since he couldn't get back to dummy for the king. Down one.

'A comedy of errors,' the prof said. 'South must cash only the A-K of trumps, then take the top clubs. When West discards, South leads a spade.'

All's well that ends well. If West leads a diamond next, South takes the jack and ace and reaches dummy with the ten of trumps to pitch a club on the diamond king. If instead West leads a spade, South ruffs in dummy and throws a club.

Bidding Quiz

YOU HOLD: ♠ A 3 ♡ 10 6 2 ◇ K 5 3 ♣ A K 8 7 4. Your partner opens one heart, you respond two clubs, he bids two diamonds and you jump to three hearts. Partner next bids four diamonds. What do you say?

ANSWER: If partner wanted to play in four hearts, he'd have bid it; his four diamonds is a cuebid that promises the ace of diamonds and suggests slam. Cooperate by cuebidding four spades, showing an ace as cheaply as you can.

22. November 9 — Exact Hindsight

North dealer
Both vulnerable

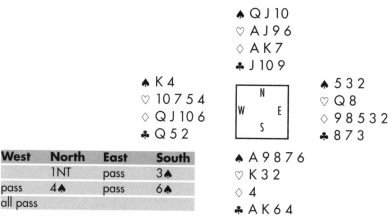

```
                    ♠ Q J 10
                    ♡ A J 9 6
                    ◇ A K 7
                    ♣ J 10 9
        ♠ K 4                      ♠ 5 3 2
        ♡ 10 7 5 4      N          ♡ Q 8
        ◇ Q J 10 6   W     E       ◇ 9 8 5 3 2
        ♣ Q 5 2         S          ♣ 8 7 3
                    ♠ A 9 8 7 6
                    ♡ K 3 2
                    ◇ 4
                    ♣ A K 6 4
```

West	North	East	South
	1NT	pass	3♠
pass	4♠	pass	6♠
all pass			

Opening lead: ◇Q

'They say the best coaches are always sitting in the stands,' a player at the club sighed. 'I think they're always sitting across from me.

'We got to a good slam,' he went on, 'but I took the ace of diamonds and lost the trump finesse. When another diamond came back, I threw a heart on the king, drew trumps and let the jack of clubs ride. Down one.

'Sure enough, the guy sitting across the table insisted the slam was cold. Hindsight is an exact science, isn't it?'

So is foresight. South must ruff the second diamond. He next draws trumps and takes the K-A of hearts. If both defenders played low, South would discard his last heart on the king of diamonds and finesse in clubs. But when East's queen of hearts falls, South can finesse with the nine next and throw two clubs on the king of diamonds and the jack of hearts.

Yes, a super-expert East could drop the queen of hearts under the ace from Q-10-8 when he had the queen of clubs. If your opponents are that good, find new ones.

Bidding Quiz

YOU HOLD: ♠ 5 3 2 ♡ Q 8 ◇ 9 8 5 3 2 ♣ 8 7 3. Dealer, on your left, opens one diamond. Your partner doubles, and the next player passes. What do you say?

ANSWER: A horrible problem. Since your opponent may make overtricks in one diamond, you must bid. Some experts would try one spade, since partner probably has good support; others would bid two clubs, the bid that's less likely to excite partner. A bid of 1NT would promise a better hand.

South dealer
Both vulnerable

```
                        ♠ 10 6 3
                        ♡ 8 2
                        ◊ Q 6 5 4 3 2
                        ♣ A J
        ♠ K Q 7                         ♠ A 9 8 5 4
        ♡ Q 10 7 4      N                ♡ 9 5
        ◊ 9 8        W      E            ◊ 7
        ♣ K 9 5 4       S                ♣ Q 8 7 3 2
                        ♠ J 2
                        ♡ A K J 6 3
                        ◊ A K J 10
                        ♣ 10 6
```

West	North	East	South
			1♡
pass	1NT	pass	2◊
pass	3◊	pass	5◊
all pass			

Opening lead: ◊ 9

'My husband's such a procrastinator,' a player at my club told me, 'I tell him his ancestors came over on the Juneflower. The only thing he ever does promptly is draw trumps.'

My friend's husband took the first trump and hurriedly drew West's last trump. South then cashed the top hearts, ruffed a heart, returned a trump to his hand and ruffed a heart.

South's last heart was established, but it did him no good. If he got back to his hand by leading to his last trump, he couldn't ruff dummy's third spade. South therefore led a spade, but West won and switched to a club, assuring three tricks for the defense.

As in many deals, procrastination in drawing trumps would pay: South must start the hearts at Trick 2. He takes the A-K, ruffs a heart with the queen of trumps, leads a trump to his ten and ruffs a heart.

South then gets back to his hand with a third trump to discard dummy's jack of clubs on the good heart. He loses two spades but takes the rest.

Bidding Quiz

YOU HOLD: ♠ J 2 ♡ A K J 6 3 ◊ A K J 10 ♣ 10 6. With neither vulnerable, your partner deals and opens three clubs, and the next player passes. What do you say?

ANSWER: Pass. If partner has a typical preempt with seven clubs headed by the K-Q-J and no other high cards, he's likely to lose two spades and a club. Of course, he may take eleven tricks if he has a singleton spade, but if his clubs are weaker, you may trade a plus score for a minus by bidding.

24. November 14 —— Patience Needed: Now!

North dealer
Both vulnerable

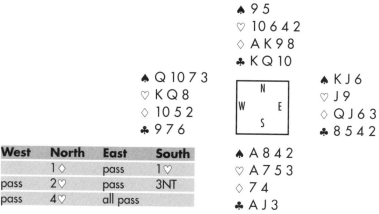

```
               ♠ 9 5
               ♡ 10 6 4 2
               ◇ A K 9 8
               ♣ K Q 10
♠ Q 10 7 3          N          ♠ K J 6
♡ K Q 8                        ♡ J 9
◇ 10 5 2     W         E       ◇ Q J 6 3
♣ 9 7 6            S           ♣ 8 5 4 2
               ♠ A 8 4 2
               ♡ A 7 5 3
               ◇ 7 4
               ♣ A J 3
```

West	North	East	South
	1◇	pass	1♡
pass	2♡	pass	3NT
pass	4♡	all pass	

Opening lead: ♠3

Unlucky Louie was late for his afternoon game, having had a medical appointment.

'Now I know why they're called "patients",' he grumbled. 'When I finally saw the doctor, he said I should have come in earlier. I told him I would have, but I'd been sitting in his waiting room for two hours.'

Louie wasn't too patient in the deal for today. East correctly played the jack on the first spade (to learn who had the queen). Louie played low, won the next spade, ruffed a spade in dummy, returned with a club and ruffed his last spade. East overruffed, and West got two trump tricks to beat the contract.

'Unlucky,' Louie shrugged. 'The defender with only three spades would usually have three trumps.'

After Louie takes the ace of spades, he must patiently lead a low trump. East wins and leads a club, and Louie wins and takes the ace of trumps. He can then ruff two spades in dummy and cash his winners in the minor suits, losing only one more trick to West's high trump.

Bidding Quiz

YOU HOLD: ♠ Q 10 7 3 ♡ K Q 8 ◇ 10 5 2 ♣ 9 7 6. Dealer, on your left, opens one heart. Your partner doubles, and the next player raises to two hearts. What do you say?

ANSWER: Bid two spades. Your partner has opening values or more with support for diamonds and clubs and good support for spades. If he has a typical minimum hand, the opponents can probably make two hearts, and you'll have an excellent chance for eight tricks in spades.

PART 5

Winter

1. November 17

West dealer
Both vulnerable

```
        ♠ A J 7 2
        ♡ J 6
        ♢ Q 7 5
        ♣ A Q 6 2

        ♠ K Q 10 9 8 3
        ♢ Q 8
        ♡ A J 3
        ♣ J 5
```

West	North	East	South
pass	1♣	pass	1♠
pass	2♠	pass	4♠
all pass			

West cashes the ace and king of hearts and shifts to a trump. Plan the play.

2. November 19

West dealer
Neither vulnerable

```
        ♠ K 5
        ♡ A K 4 2
        ♢ A 10 6 5 2
        ♣ 10 6

        ♠ 10
        ♡ J
        ♢ K 8 3
        ♣ K J 9 7 5 4 3 2
```

West	North	East	South
1♠	dbl	2♠	5♣
dbl	all pass		

West leads the seven of diamonds. Plan the play.

3. November 21   Blowing Off Esteem

South dealer
N-S vulnerable

```
            ♠ K 10 5
            ♡ 8 5
            ◇ Q 10 8 3
            ♣ K J 6 2

            ♠ A Q J 8 4
            ♡ K 6 4
            ◇ 9
            ♣ A Q 10 5
```

West	North	East	South
			1♠
2◇	2♠	pass	4♠
all pass			

West leads the king of diamonds and shifts to a trump. Plan the play.

4. November 23   Louie's Losing Game

North dealer
Neither vulnerable

```
            ♠ A 8 7 4
            ♡ A Q
            ◇ A 6 3
            ♣ 9 6 4 2

            ♠ K 10 9 6 3 2
            ♡ J 5
            ◇ K 4
            ♣ A J 10
```

West	North	East	South
	1♣	pass	1♠
pass	2♠	pass	4♠
all pass			

West leads the jack of diamonds. Since twelve tricks seem possible, it would be embarrassing to go down in game. Plan the play.

1. November 17

Wintery Tale

West dealer
Both vulnerable

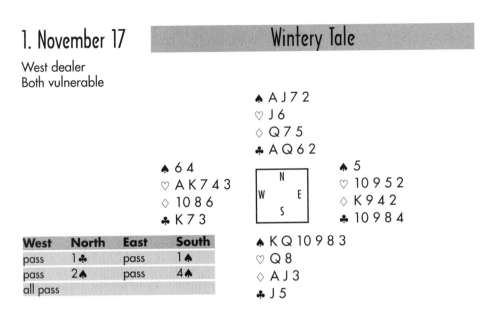

```
                 ♠ A J 7 2
                 ♡ J 6
                 ◊ Q 7 5
                 ♣ A Q 6 2
 ♠ 6 4                          ♠ 5
 ♡ A K 7 4 3          N         ♡ 10 9 5 2
 ◊ 10 8 6        W         E    ◊ K 9 4 2
 ♣ K 7 3              S         ♣ 10 9 8 4
                 ♠ K Q 10 9 8 3
                 ♡ Q 8
                 ◊ A J 3
                 ♣ J 5
```

West	North	East	South
pass	1♣	pass	1♠
pass	2♠	pass	4♠
all pass			

Opening lead: ♡A

Winter, the age of shovelry, had come again: an ice storm gripped our city, and trees glittered like crystal chandeliers. But someone had shoveled a path to the bridge club's front door, and inside, the penny Chicago game went on.

After taking two hearts, West led a trump. South drew trumps and next made the chivalrous-looking play of a club from dummy to his jack.

'Thanks,' West chortled as he took the king. 'You could've won a finesse if you weren't so sporting.' When West returned a club, South took the A-Q, throwing a diamond, led a diamond to his jack and claimed. Was his play chivalrous or shrewd?

South knew East had at least one king; West hadn't opened the bidding but had played the A-K of hearts. If West had the king of clubs, South would surely make the contract since the diamond finesse would work.

If instead East had held the king of clubs, he'd have had to take it or lose it. But then South would score the jack of clubs and later pitch two diamonds on the A-Q.

Bidding Quiz

YOU HOLD: ♠ 6 4 ♡ A K 7 4 3 ◊ 10 8 6 ♣ K 7 3. Your partner opens one spade, you bid two hearts, he rebids two spades and you try 2NT. Partner next bids three diamonds. What do you say?

ANSWER: Your 2NT was no thing of beauty; a pass would have been a sound option. Partner's third bid suggests six spades, four diamonds and minimum values. (If he had extra strength, he'd have bid two diamonds or three spades at his second turn.) Return to three spades.

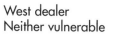

West dealer
Neither vulnerable

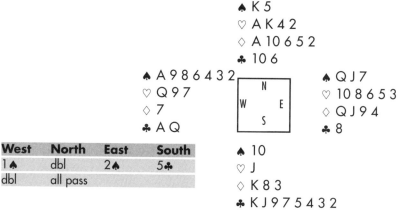

```
              ♠ K 5
              ♡ A K 4 2
              ◇ A 10 6 5 2
              ♣ 10 6
♠ A 9 8 6 4 3 2          ♠ Q J 7
♡ Q 9 7        N        ♡ 10 8 6 5 3
◇ 7       W        E     ◇ Q J 9 4
♣ A Q          S        ♣ 8
              ♠ 10
              ♡ J
              ◇ K 8 3
              ♣ K J 9 7 5 4 3 2
```

West	North	East	South
1♠	dbl	2♠	5♣
dbl	all pass		

Opening lead: ◇7

'I figured if I played on a team with the Halo,' Unlucky Louie told me, 'some of his luck might rub off.' Louie was referring to Harlow the Halo, whose luck is as good as Louie's is awful.

'The contract was five clubs at both tables of our match,' Louie said, 'but when I was West, I led the ace of spades, and declarer had no chance.

'At the other table,' Louie went on, 'Harlow was South, and West misjudged by leading a diamond. Harlow took the king, cashed the A-K of hearts to pitch a spade — and then led a trump. West took the queen and ace and led the queen of hearts, and Harlow had to lose a diamond.'

'His corn is always ripe,' I observed, 'but he often neglects the harvest.'

'If Harlow ruffs a heart at Trick 4 and leads the king of trumps,' Louie sighed, 'West is endplayed. If he leads the ace of spades, Harlow ruffs and later throws a diamond on the king of spades.'

It seems that even with Harlow on his side, the best Louie can hope for is to break even.

Bidding Quiz

YOU HOLD: ♠ K 5 ♡ A K 4 2 ◇ A 10 6 5 2 ♣ 10 6. You open one diamond, and your partner bids one spade. The opponents pass. What do you say?

ANSWER: You can't rebid two diamonds with a poor five-card suit or 'reverse' with two hearts, which would promise more strength. Bid 1 NT, suggesting minimum values with balanced pattern. Some players would have opened one heart to handle this problem, but that 'solution' also has its flaws.

Blowing Off Esteem

South dealer
N-S vulnerable

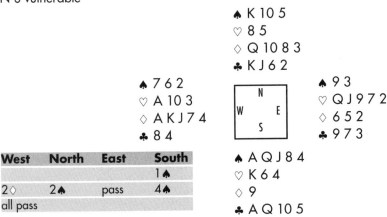

```
              ♠ K 10 5
              ♡ 8 5
              ◇ Q 10 8 3
              ♣ K J 6 2

♠ 7 6 2                    ♠ 9 3
♡ A 10 3         N         ♡ Q J 9 7 2
◇ A K J 7 4   W     E      ◇ 6 5 2
♣ 8 4            S         ♣ 9 7 3

              ♠ A Q J 8 4
              ♡ K 6 4
              ◇ 9
              ♣ A Q 10 5
```

West	North	East	South
			1♠
2◇	2♠	pass	4♠
all pass			

Opening lead: ◇K

'I was up against S— ,' a club player told me, naming a member who is always blowing off esteem: he not only calls himself an expert but is sure the rest of our members have the skills of a rock.

'He was South,' my friend said, 'and I shifted to a trump at Trick 2. He won in his hand and led a low heart, and East won and led another trump. South won in dummy and tried a heart to his king, but I won and led a third trump. He lost another heart, went down and said he was unlucky.'

'Did you tell him four spades was cold?' I asked.

'No, but North sure did. After I shifted to a trump, South could draw trumps, cash the A-Q-J of clubs, lead the queen of diamonds from dummy and pitch a heart. I'd have to win and lead either the jack of diamonds, making dummy's ten high, or a heart, letting the king score.'

'Did South show any sign of humility?' I asked.

'Let's put it this way. It'll be a while before he calls Dial-a-Prayer to see if he has any messages.'

Bidding Quiz

YOU HOLD: ♠ A Q J 8 4 ♡ K 6 4 ◇ 9 ♣ A Q 10 5. You open one spade, and your partner bids two hearts. The opponents pass. What do you say?

ANSWER: Since partner promises five or more hearts, you could bid four hearts. A better way to describe the hand is to bid three clubs, then support hearts. You'll suggest slam (since you failed to bid game immediately) and a singleton diamond. Let partner decide whether he has the right cards for slam.

4. November 23   Louie's Losing Game

North dealer
Neither vulnerable

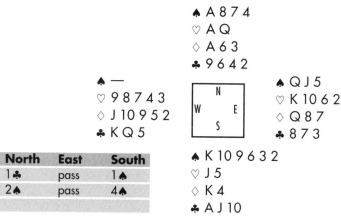

```
                    ♠ A 8 7 4
                    ♡ A Q
                    ◇ A 6 3
                    ♣ 9 6 4 2
♠ —                                    ♠ Q J 5
♡ 9 8 7 4 3          N                 ♡ K 10 6 2
◇ J 10 9 5 2     W       E             ◇ Q 8 7
♣ K Q 5              S                 ♣ 8 7 3
                    ♠ K 10 9 6 3 2
                    ♡ J 5
                    ◇ K 4
                    ♣ A J 10
```

West	North	East	South
	1♣	pass	1♠
pass	2♠	pass	4♠
all pass			

Opening lead: ◇ J

In a contest between Unlucky Louie and the world, I'd always bet on the world.

'How many tricks would you expect at a spade contract?' Louie asked me, showing the North-South cards. Twelve looked possible, but before I could say so, Louie was telling me how he wound up with nine.

'I took the king of diamonds,' he said, 'and the king of trumps. When West showed out, I led a trump to the ace and tried a club to my ten. West won and shifted to a heart.

'When I finessed with dummy's queen, East won, cashed his high trump and led another club. I had to finesse with the jack, but I knew it would lose — and it did. Down one.'

'Hold it,' I said. 'If the contract is only four spades, all bets are off.'

How do you play to assure just ten tricks?

After Louie cashes the top trumps, he should take the ace of diamonds and ruff a diamond. He then cashes the ace of hearts and exits with the queen. East can win and lead a club, but Louie ducks, and when West wins, he is endplayed.

Bidding Quiz

YOU HOLD: ♠ A 8 7 4 ♡ A Q ◇ A 6 3 ♣ 9 6 4 2. Dealer, on your right, opens one heart. You double, and your partner bids two spades. The opponents pass. What do you say?

ANSWER: This decision is close. Your partner's jump response is invitational to game; he may have as few as 9 points and surely has no more than 11. You have 14 points, but your hand is worth more because the queen of hearts is surely a winner. Hence raise to three spades.

5. November 25 — Minnie's Mighty Pin

South dealer
Both vulnerable

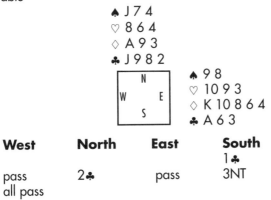

```
              ♠ J 7 4
              ♡ 8 6 4
              ◊ A 9 3
              ♣ J 9 8 2
                            ♠ 9 8
          N                 ♡ 10 9 3
       W     E              ◊ K 10 8 6 4
          S                 ♣ A 6 3
```

West	North	East	South
			1♣
pass	2♣	pass	3NT
all pass			

West leads the deuce of hearts. South takes your nine with the queen and leads the king of clubs. You play low, and on the next club West discards the six of spades. How do you defend?

6. November 27 — Thanksgiving Turkey

North dealer
N-S vulnerable

```
              ♠ K Q J 8
              ♡ K J 9
              ◊ 10 5
              ♣ A K J 4


              ♠ 7 5
              ♡ A Q 10 7 4
              ◊ J 9 8 6
              ♣ Q 6
```

West	North	East	South
	1♣	pass	1♡
pass	2♠(!)	pass	3◊
pass	4♡	pass	4NT
pass	5◊	pass	5♡
all pass			

West leads the ten of clubs. Plan the play.

7. November 28   Shop Early

South dealer
Both vulnerable

```
              ♠ Q J 10
              ♡ 5 3
              ◊ Q 10 7 6 2
              ♣ K 7 2

              ♠ A K 9 8 3
              ♡ A Q 9 6 2
              ◊ 8 3
              ♣ A
```

West	North	East	South
			1♠
pass	2♠	pass	4♠
all pass			

West leads a trump, and East follows. Plan the play.

8. December 1   Fear Not

South dealer
N-S vulnerable

```
              ♠ Q 9 8 2
              ♡ A 7 2
              ◊ 7 6 4 3
              ♣ Q 5

              ♠ A J 10 7 5
              ♡ K 6 4
              ◊ A 2
              ♣ A 8 2
```

West	North	East	South
			1♠
pass	2♠	pass	3♠
pass	4♠	all pass	

West leads the jack of hearts. Plan the play.

South dealer
Both vulnerable

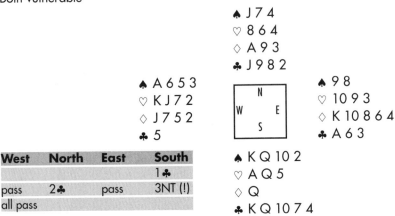

```
                        ♠ J 7 4
                        ♡ 8 6 4
                        ◇ A 9 3
                        ♣ J 9 8 2
        ♠ A 6 5 3                      ♠ 9 8
        ♡ K J 7 2          N           ♡ 10 9 3
        ◇ J 7 5 2      W       E       ◇ K 10 8 6 4
        ♣ 5                S           ♣ A 6 3
                        ♠ K Q 10 2
                        ♡ A Q 5
                        ◇ Q
                        ♣ K Q 10 7 4
```

West	North	East	South
			1♣
pass	2♣	pass	3NT (!)
all pass			

Opening lead: ♡2

'I'd have gotten away with it against anyone else,' Cy the Cynic told me. 'Confound Minnie and her glasses!'

Cy meant our senior member Minnie Bottoms; her old bifocals make her mix up kings and jacks, often to an opponent's dismay. The deal arose in a duplicate game, and Cy, South, had gambled with his jump to 3NT.

'I took the queen of hearts,' Cy said, 'and started the clubs. Minnie won the second club, as West threw a spade, and shifted to the king of diamonds! She thought she had J-10-8-6-4, of course. She pinned my queen and I went down two. If she returns a heart, I can scrape home.

'What bothers me,' Cy said, 'is that when Minnie led the king of diamonds, I heard her mumble "The pin is mightier than the sword".'

The king of diamonds is East's proper lead. East knows West had a singleton club and led from a four-card heart suit. If West had five spades, he'd have led a spade, so West has at least four diamonds and South has one.

Is Minnie fooling us all?

Bidding Quiz

YOU HOLD: ♠ 9 8 ♡ 10 9 3 ◇ K 10 8 6 4 ♣ A 6 3. Your partner opens one diamond, you raise to two diamonds and he then bids two spades. The opponents pass. What do you say?

ANSWER: Although you have only 7 points in high cards, this is a promising hand with five good trumps, a side ace and a probable ruffing feature in spades. Bid three clubs, suggesting club strength. Whether partner returns to three diamonds next or tries 3NT, you'll pass.

6. November 27   Thanksgiving Turkey

North dealer
N-S vulnerable

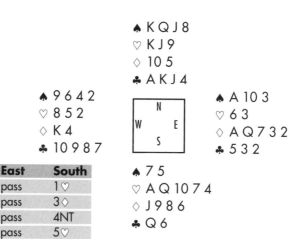

```
              ♠ K Q J 8
              ♡ K J 9
              ◇ 10 5
              ♣ A K J 4
♠ 9 6 4 2                    ♠ A 10 3
♡ 8 5 2          N           ♡ 6 3
◇ K 4       W        E       ◇ A Q 7 3 2
♣ 10 9 8 7       S           ♣ 5 3 2
              ♠ 7 5
              ♡ A Q 10 7 4
              ◇ J 9 8 6
              ♣ Q 6
```

West	North	East	South
	1♣	pass	1♡
pass	2♠(!)	pass	3◇
pass	4◇	pass	4NT
pass	5◇	pass	5♡
all pass			

Opening lead: ♣10

'Do you know how to keep a turkey in suspense?' Unlucky Louie asked me.

'No,' I replied innocently. 'How?'

There was an ever-lengthening silence. When I finally caught on, Louie roared with laughter.

A little later, I watched as North-South climbed indiscreetly up to five hearts. Louie, sitting West, led the ten of clubs. After giving thanks that Louie hadn't led a diamond, South won with the queen and cashed the nine and jack of trumps.

South then took three more clubs, pitching his two low spades as Louie had to follow suit. South next led the king of spades from dummy, and when East's ace covered, South ruffed, got back to dummy with the king of trumps and threw two diamonds on the Q-J of spades. South conceded two diamonds and sat back to listen to East lecture Louie on opening leads.

'Do you know what a bridge expert has for Thanksgiving dinner?' I asked Louie after all the shouting had died down.

'No.'

'I didn't think so,' I said.

Bidding Quiz

YOU HOLD: ♠ A 10 3 ♡ 6 3 ◇ A Q 7 3 2 ♣ 5 3 2. Your partner opens 2NT, and the next player passes. What do you say?

ANSWER: The answer depends on your partnership's range for a 2NT opening. If partner promises 22 to 24 points, bid 6NT; but if he promises 21 or 22 points, raise to 4NT, a 'quantitative' try for slam (not the Blackwood convention). Since your hand is worth 11 points, you want to be in slam only if he has maximum values.

Shop Early

South dealer
Both vulnerable

```
                    ♠ Q J 10
                    ♡ 5 3
                    ◇ Q 10 7 6 2
                    ♣ K 7 2
   ♠ 7 6 5                          ♠ 4 2
   ♡ K J 10 8          N            ♡ 7 4
   ◇ K 5         W           E      ◇ A J 9 4
   ♣ Q 8 6 4          S            ♣ J 10 9 5 3
                    ♠ A K 9 8 3
                    ♡ A Q 9 6 2
                    ◇ 8 3
                    ♣ A
```

West	North	East	South
			1♠
pass	2♠	pass	4♠
all pass			

Opening lead: ♠7

'Each year the stores put up their Christmas decorations closer to Thanksgiving,' a player at the club observed.

'Tell me about it,' Cy the Cynic muttered. 'The other day I saw a turkey in a pear tree.'

South won the trump opening lead and hastened to get rid of a diamond loser. He took the ace of clubs, led a trump to dummy and threw a diamond on the king of clubs. South next led a heart to the queen, but West won and led his last trump. South then led the ace and a low heart, but West got two more hearts, and East got a diamond. Down one.

It's fine to do your Christmas shopping early (it gets you in shape for those January sales), but South was too quick to seek a discard; he should finesse in hearts at Trick 2. West takes the king but is sure to lead another trump. South wins, takes the ace of clubs and the ace of hearts, and ruffs a heart. He throws a diamond on the king of clubs, ruffs a club and draws trumps. South then concedes a heart and loses two hearts and one diamond.

Bidding Quiz

YOU HOLD: ♠ 4 2 ♡ 7 4 ◇ A J 9 4 ♣ J 10 9 5 3. Your partner opens one club, you raise to two clubs and he bids 2NT. The opponents pass. What do you say?

ANSWER: Partner has a strong hand; he bid 2NT to try for game, not to escape from clubs. (Without game interest, he should pass regardless of his club holding.) Since you have a minimum raise, you can't bid game; but since your hand is distributional, you should return to three clubs.

8. December 1

South dealer
N-S vulnerable

```
              ♠ Q 9 8 2
              ♡ A 7 2
              ◇ 7 6 4 3
              ♣ Q 5
♠ K 4                        ♠ 6 3
♡ J 10 8 3        N          ♡ Q 9 5
◇ K J 8 5     W       E      ◇ Q 10 9
♣ K 7 4           S          ♣ J 10 9 6 3
              ♠ A J 10 7 5
              ♡ K 6 4
              ◇ A 2
              ♣ A 8 2
```

West	North	East	South
			1♠
pass	2♠	pass	3♠
pass	4♠	all pass	

Opening lead: ♡ J

'Christmas is getting so expensive it scares me,' a club player remarked between deals. 'Santa's aliases ought to be Saint Nick, Kris Kringle and American Express.'

'You're scared of Christmas?' I marvelled.

'A clear case of Claus-trophobia,' a kibitzer chuckled.

South's play of the next deal suggested he was afraid of more than just Christmas. He took the ace of hearts and lost a trump finesse. West led another heart, and South eventually lost a trick in each suit.

Show me a man who's afraid of Christmas, and I'll show you Noel Coward; and show me a declarer who's afraid to wait to draw trumps, and I'll show you one who goes down when he shouldn't. South must win the first heart with the king to lead a low club toward the queen. He can't lead trumps yet; getting a discard for his heart loser is more urgent.

When West takes the king of clubs and leads another heart, South wins, cashes the queen of clubs, returns a trump to the ace and throws dummy's last heart on the ace of clubs.

Bidding Quiz

YOU HOLD: ♠ K 4 ♡ J 10 8 3 ◇ K J 8 5 ♣ K 7 4. You pass as dealer, the next player passes and your partner opens one spade. The next player passes. What do you say?

ANSWER: Bid 2NT. If you hadn't passed originally, this bid would be forcing and would promise 13 to 15 points, balanced distribution and a certain trick in each of the unbid suits. After you've passed, you promise the same type of hand with only 11 or 12 points.

9. December 6

South dealer
Both vulnerable

```
            ♠ Q 7 4
            ♡ A J 5
            ◇ A Q 10 7 3
            ♣ 7 4

            ♠ A 6
            ♡ K Q 7
            ◇ J 9 6
            ♣ K Q 9 5 3
```

West	North	East	South
			1♣
pass	1◇	pass	1NT
pass	3NT	all pass	

West leads the five of spades. You play low from dummy and take East's ten with the ace. When you let the nine of diamonds ride, East takes the king and returns the deuce of clubs to the king and ace. West then leads the jack of spades. What do you play from dummy?

10. December 8

South dealer
N-S vulnerable

```
            ♠ 7
            ♡ 10 8 4 2
            ◇ A Q 10 4 3 2
            ♣ A 7

            ♠ A K 8 5 4
            ♡ K Q 7 5 3
            ◇ —
            ♣ K 6 3
```

West	North	East	South
			1♠
pass	2◇	pass	2♡
pass	4♡	pass	4♠
pass	5♣	pass	6♡
all pass			

West leads the eight of diamonds. Plan the play.

11. December 11   Subordinated Thinking

South dealer
Neither vulnerable

```
              ♠ Q 7 6
              ♡ 9 6 5
              ◇ K Q 10 8 6
              ♣ 6 2

              ♠ K J 3
              ♡ A K 2
              ◇ J 5 4
              ♣ A K J 8
```

West	North	East	South
			1♣
pass	1◇	pass	2NT
pass	3NT	all pass	

West leads the ten of spades, East plays low and your king wins. You lead a diamond: nine, king, three. How do you continue?

12. December 13   Make Your Own Luck

South dealer
N-S vulnerable

```
              ♠ K 7 2
              ♡ 5 4 3
              ◇ A 9 7 5 3
              ♣ A J

              ♠ A Q J 10 8
              ♡ A Q 2
              ◇ 8 2
              ♣ 9 6 4
```

West	North	East	South
			1♠
2♣	2◇	pass	2♠
pass	4♠	all pass	

West leads the king of clubs, and you take dummy's ace. Plan the play.

South dealer
Both vulnerable

```
                    ♠ Q 7 4
                    ♡ A J 5
                    ◇ A Q 10 7 3
                    ♣ 7 4
        ♠ J 9 8 5 2            ♠ K 10 3
        ♡ 10 6 2      N       ♡ 9 8 4 3
        ◇ 5 4 2    W     E    ◇ K 8
        ♣ A 10        S       ♣ J 8 6 2
                    ♠ A 6
                    ♡ K Q 7
                    ◇ J 9 6
                    ♣ K Q 9 5 3
```

West	North	East	South
			1♣
pass	1◇	pass	1NT
pass	3NT	all pass	

Opening lead: ♠5

'Got your Christmas tree up and trimmed?' I asked Cy the Cynic.

'Not yet,' Cy said. 'Some of my lights are on the blink, so to speak. I'm testing them all.'

'Does it take so long?' I asked.

'I do it,' the Cynic sighed, 'by process of illumination.'

Illuminating things happen in the play of every deal. In this deal declarer plays low from dummy on the first spade and takes East's ten with the ace. South then leads the nine of diamonds to finesse.

East wins and returns a club to the king and ace, and West then leads the jack of spades. Should South play low from dummy, hoping to block the spades, or cover with the queen?

South can shed some light on the matter by putting himself in East's place. If West had the king of spades, East would surely return a spade at Trick 3 to let West set up his suit while he had the ace of clubs for an entry.

South must play low from dummy on the second spade. The defense takes two spades, but South has the rest.

Bidding Quiz

YOU HOLD: ♠ Q 7 4 ♡ A J 5 ◇ A Q 10 7 3 ♣ 7 4. You open one diamond, your partner bids one heart and the next player bids one spade. What do you say?

ANSWER: Your opening bid was a minimum, and your opponent's overcall has done little to improve it. Since you have nothing you're eager to say, pass. If your opponent had passed, you'd have raised to two hearts, but you needn't raise with only three-card support when a pass is a sound option.

10. December 8 | Unguided Missile

South dealer
N-S vulnerable

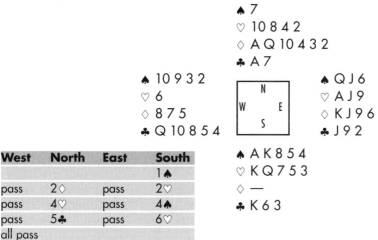

```
                  ♠ 7
                  ♡ 10 8 4 2
                  ◇ A Q 10 4 3 2
                  ♣ A 7
   ♠ 10 9 3 2              ♠ Q J 6
   ♡ 6            N        ♡ A J 9
   ◇ 8 7 5    W      E     ◇ K J 9 6
   ♣ Q 10 8 5 4    S       ♣ J 9 2
                  ♠ A K 8 5 4
                  ♡ K Q 7 5 3
                  ◇ —
                  ♣ K 6 3
```

West	North	East	South
			1♠
pass	2◇	pass	2♡
pass	4♡	pass	4♠
pass	5♣	pass	6♡
all pass			

Opening lead: ◇ 8

Our manager had hung sprigs of mistletoe about the club in deference to the holiday season.

'I wonder,' mused a player in a game I was kibitzing, 'if athletes have athlete's foot, do astronauts have missile toe?'

'Can't say,' his partner replied, 'but you surely played that last hand like an unguided missile.'

South threw a spade on the ace of diamonds and led a trump to his king. He cashed the A-K of spades, ruffed a spade, took the top clubs, ruffed a club, ruffed a diamond and ruffed his last low spade. East overruffed with the jack and won the setting trick with the ace.

'It's no help to cash only one top spade before I ruff spades,' South noted. 'I still lose two trumps.'

South's error came early; at Trick 1 he pitches a club, not the fifth spade (which may be a winner). South next leads a trump to his king, takes the ace of spades, ruffs a spade, comes to the king of clubs and ruffs a spade. He then leads a trump and loses only to the ace of trumps.

Bidding Quiz

YOU HOLD: ♠ Q J 6 ♡ A J 9 ◇ K J 9 6 ♣ J 9 2. Your partner opens one heart, you respond 2NT (13 to 15 points) and he next bids three clubs. The opponents pass. What do you say?

ANSWER: Bid three hearts. Your duty is to show your support for partner's major suit. If his distribution is semibalanced, he may try 3NT next to give you a choice of games, and you'll pass. If you bid 3NT now, however, you'll be telling the same story twice.

Subordinated Thinking

South dealer
Neither vulnerable

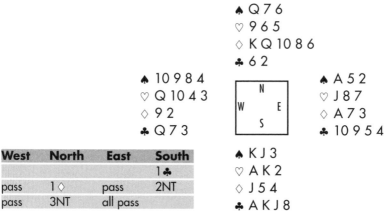

```
                        ♠ Q 7 6
                        ♡ 9 6 5
                        ◇ K Q 10 8 6
                        ♣ 6 2
        ♠ 10 9 8 4                      ♠ A 5 2
        ♡ Q 10 4 3         N            ♡ J 8 7
        ◇ 9 2        W          E       ◇ A 7 3
        ♣ Q 7 3            S            ♣ 10 9 5 4
                        ♠ K J 3
                        ♡ A K 2
                        ◇ J 5 4
                        ♣ A K J 8
```

West	North	East	South
			1♣
pass	1◇	pass	2NT
pass	3NT	all pass	

Opening lead: ♠10

My friend the English professor was spending some Christmas vacation time at the bridge club.

'Santa got his elves making something for you this year?' I asked.

'In my line of work, we call them subordinate Clauses,' he remarked with a twinkle.

The professor was declarer in this deal. East refused the first spade (so dummy's queen wouldn't be an entry to the diamonds), and the prof won with the king and led a diamond. West signalled with the nine and East ducked. The prof next led a club — and played the eight. When West won with the queen, South finished with three clubs, two diamonds, two hearts and two spades.

The prof feared East could hold up the ace of diamonds twice, isolating the diamonds. Then declarer would need three club tricks.

To finesse with the jack on the first club would be an inferior play — or a subordinate play, if you will. South could always finesse with the jack later; the deep finesse, hoping East had the 10-9, gave him an extra chance.

Bidding Quiz

YOU HOLD: ♠ Q 7 6 ♡ 9 6 5 ◇ K Q 10 8 6 ♣ 6 2. Dealer, on your left, opens one spade. Your partner doubles, and the next player passes. What do you say?

ANSWER: Bid 1NT, promising 6 to 9 points, balanced distribution and a trick in spades. A bid of two diamonds would not be a terrible goof, but you'd make that bid with no strength. The encouraging 1NT response is your best chance to get to the most likely game.

12. December 13 | Make Your Own Luck

South dealer
N-S vulnerable

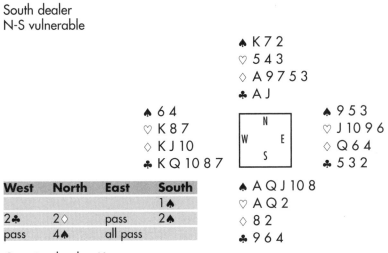

```
                    ♠ K 7 2
                    ♡ 5 4 3
                    ◇ A 9 7 5 3
                    ♣ A J
        ♠ 6 4                       ♠ 9 5 3
        ♡ K 8 7          N          ♡ J 10 9 6
        ◇ K J 10      W     E       ◇ Q 6 4
        ♣ K Q 10 8 7     S          ♣ 5 3 2
                    ♠ A Q J 10 8
                    ♡ A Q 2
                    ◇ 8 2
                    ♣ 9 6 4
```

West	North	East	South
			1♠
2♣	2◇	pass	2♠
pass	4♠	all pass	

Opening lead: ♣K

'Santa going to fill your stocking this year?' I asked Unlucky Louie, who seemed a little dispirited.

'He won't get a chance,' Louie sighed. 'I have a hang-up about Christmas stockings, if you'll pardon the phrase, but maybe he'll leave me some good luck under the tree.'

Louie, South, won the first club and led a low diamond from dummy. West won, cashed the queen of clubs and led the ten. Louie ruffed in dummy, drew trumps, led to the ace of diamonds and tried a heart to his queen. West won, and East got a heart later. Down one.

'I wanted to set up the diamonds,' Louie said, 'but when the man led the third club, he killed my late entry to dummy.'

Louie makes his own luck by pitching a heart from dummy on the third club. If West then leads a trump, Louie wins, takes the ace of diamonds and ruffs a diamond. When diamonds break 3-3, he draw trumps with the A-K and throws two hearts on the good diamonds.

If diamonds split 4-2, Louie can try the heart finesse for his tenth trick.

Bidding Quiz

YOU HOLD: ♠ A Q J 10 8 ♡ A Q 2 ◇ 8 2 ♣ 9 6 4. You open one spade, and your partner responds two hearts. The opponents pass. What do you say?

ANSWER: Bid three hearts. This is one time you can happily raise with only three trumps. Partner will never respond two hearts to one spade with only four hearts, since he'd always have an option: a spade raise, a 2NT response or a temporizing bid in a minor suit (in a pinch, even a three-card minor).

13. December 15   Trimming the Defense

East dealer
E-W vulnerable

      ♠ K J
      ♡ J 9 8 4 3
      ◇ K 7 6 3
      ♣ 7 4

      ♠ 9
      ♡ K Q 10 6 2
      ◇ A J 9 4
      ♣ K J 5

West	North	East	South
		1♠	2♡
2♠	3♡	pass	4♡
all pass			

West leads the deuce of spades. East wins with the queen and leads the ace, and you ruff. You lead a trump, and West takes the ace and shifts helpfully to a club. East takes the ace and returns a club, and you win and draw trumps (West started with A-5). When you ruff your jack of clubs in dummy, East discards. How do you play the diamonds?

14. December 17   Christmas Cards

South dealer
Both vulnerable

      ♠ 7 4
      ♡ J 9 2
      ◇ K Q 6 2
      ♣ A 10 9 4

      ♠ A 9 8 3
      ♡ A Q
      ◇ A 5 3
      ♣ Q J 8 2

West	North	East	South
			1NT
pass	3NT	all pass	

West leads the king of spades. You play low twice and win the third spade, on which East discards a heart. Plan the play.

15. December 19

South dealer
Both vulnerable

```
              ♠ K J 10 6 5 3
              ♡ A 6
              ◇ 4 3
              ♣ 7 5 4

              ♠ A
              ♡ K 9 8 7 4 2
              ◇ A K Q J
              ♣ A Q
```

West	North	East	South
			2♣
pass	2♠	pass	3♡
pass	3♠	pass	3NT
pass	4♡	pass	6NT
all pass			

West leads the ten of diamonds. Plan the play.

16. December 20

East dealer
Both vulnerable

```
              ♠ Q 10
              ♡ 10 8 7 5
              ◇ A K J
              ♣ K J 9 7

              ♠ 7 4
              ♡ K Q J 9 6 3
              ◇ Q 10 9 5 4
              ♣ —
```

West	North	East	South
		1♠	2♡
2♠	4♡	dbl	all pass

West leads the deuce of spades. East wins with the jack and shifts to the six of diamonds.
Plan the play.

13. December 15 — Trimming the Defense

East dealer
E-W vulnerable

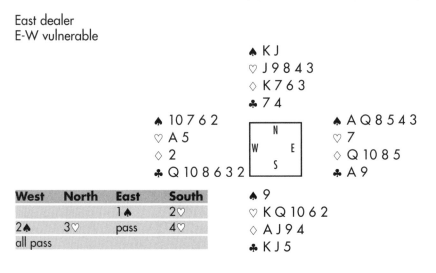

♠ K J
♡ J 9 8 4 3
◊ K 7 6 3
♣ 7 4

♠ 10 7 6 2   ♠ A Q 8 5 4 3
♡ A 5   ♡ 7
◊ 2   ◊ Q 10 8 5
♣ Q 10 8 6 3 2   ♣ A 9

♠ 9
♡ K Q 10 6 2
◊ A J 9 4
♣ K J 5

West	North	East	South
		1♠	2♡
2♠	3♡	pass	4♡
all pass			

Opening lead: ♠2

'Did you ever get your Christmas tree up and trimmed?' I asked Cy the Cynic between deals.

'It's just a scraggly pine,' said Cy, 'and all I used to decorate it was a shotgun shell. I now have a cartridge in a bare tree.'

I resisted an urge to conk him and instead went out to get him in this deal. I was South, and we managed to buy the deal at four hearts when Cy was cowed by the vulnerability. I ruffed the second spade and forced out the ace of trumps. West next led a club, and Cy, East, took the ace and returned a club.

I drew trumps and ruffed a club. When Cy discarded, I knew he'd started with two clubs, one heart and six spades (West had led the deuce, suggesting four, and if Cy had held seven spades, even he would have bid more); hence four diamonds. I took the king of diamonds, finessed with the nine, returned a trump to dummy, led a diamond to the jack and claimed.

'We'd make five spades,' Cy said dazedly.

'It serves you right,' I told him, 'for cracking such bad jokes.'

Bidding Quiz

YOU HOLD: ♠ 9 ♡ K Q 10 6 2 ◊ A J 9 4 ♣ K J 5. Dealer, on your right, opens one spade. What do you say?

ANSWER: Bid two hearts. The problem with a takeout double is that if partner responds in clubs or notrump, you don't have enough strength to bid two hearts next; hence you may miss a 5-3 heart fit. If instead you bid two hearts, the next player raises to two spades and two passes follow, you'll double (for takeout).

14. December 17

South dealer
Both vulnerable

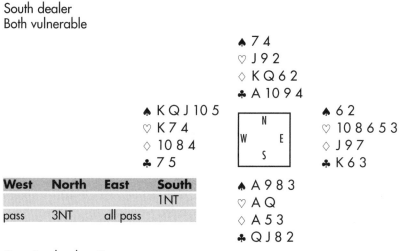

```
                    ♠ 7 4
                    ♡ J 9 2
                    ◇ K Q 6 2
                    ♣ A 10 9 4
  ♠ K Q J 10 5              ♠ 6 2
  ♡ K 7 4          N        ♡ 10 8 6 5 3
  ◇ 10 8 4     W       E    ◇ J 9 7
  ♣ 7 5            S        ♣ K 6 3
                    ♠ A 9 8 3
                    ♡ A Q
                    ◇ A 5 3
                    ♣ Q J 8 2
```

West	North	East	South
			1NT
pass	3NT	all pass	

Opening lead: ♠K

'By the time the last ribbon on the last package is tied,' a club player told me, 'I'm fit to be. But at least I made sure our Christmas cards got sent. Last year I gave them to my husband, who never mailed them.'

'What was your plan?' I asked.

'I sent one to myself. When it didn't come, I started asking questions.'

Today's declarer didn't plan ahead quite as well. He won the third spade and let the queen of clubs ride. East took the king and led a heart.

South had three clubs, three diamonds, a heart and a spade. He could get a ninth trick if the heart finesse won or if the diamonds broke 3-3, but couldn't try both chances. Inevitably, he finessed in hearts, the better percentage play, and went down.

To try all his chances, South must cash the king, queen and ace of diamonds before he finesses in clubs. If diamonds break badly and the club finesse loses, South will finesse in hearts as his last chance. But when diamonds break 3-3, South has his nine tricks.

Bidding Quiz

YOU HOLD: ♠ A 9 8 3 ♡ A Q ◇ A 5 3 ♣ Q J 8 2. You open 1NT, and your partner bids three spades. You raise to four spades, and he next tries five clubs. What do you say?

ANSWER: Since you have sound values and good spade support, you might have tried an 'advance cuebid' of four diamonds instead of bidding four spades. You must certainly make sure of slam now. Bid six spades or, to start the search for a grand slam, cuebid five diamonds.

15. December 19 — He Yam What He Yam

South dealer
Both vulnerable

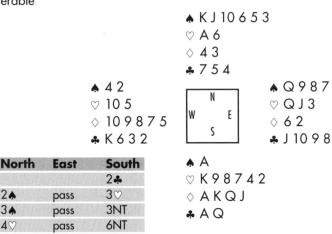

```
                       ♠ K J 10 6 5 3
                       ♡ A 6
                       ◊ 4 3
                       ♣ 7 5 4
         ♠ 4 2                            ♠ Q 9 8 7
         ♡ 10 5            N              ♡ Q J 3
         ◊ 10 9 8 7 5   W     E           ◊ 6 2
         ♣ K 6 3 2         S              ♣ J 10 9 8
                       ♠ A
                       ♡ K 9 8 7 4 2
                       ◊ A K Q J
                       ♣ A Q
```

West	North	East	South
			2♣
pass	2♠	pass	3♡
pass	3♠	pass	3NT
pass	4♡	pass	6NT
all pass			

Opening lead: ◊ 10

Unlucky Louie had begun to resemble a candied yam, a fact he attributed to attending too many holiday parties.

'I feel like I've been on a cruise ship since the first of the month,' Louie told me. 'What I need is a bathroom scale that's seasonally adjusted.'

Louie's play in this slam needed some adjustment that wasn't seasonal. After taking the first trick, he unblocked the ace of spades, led a heart to dummy's ace and tried the king of spades. When the queen didn't fall, Louie returned a heart to his king and conceded a heart. Alas, East won and cashed the queen of spades for the setting trick.

At any time of the year, South should lead a low heart at Trick 3 — but he should play low from dummy. If East returns the jack of clubs, South takes the ace, leads a heart to the ace and cashes the king of spades, discarding the queen of clubs.

South then returns to his hand and runs the hearts, winning two spades, five hearts, four diamonds and a club.

Bidding Quiz

YOU HOLD: ♠ K J 10 6 5 3 ♡ A 6 ◊ 4 3 ♣ 7 5 4. Your partner bids 1NT, and the next player passes. What do you say?

ANSWER: You must insist on game: your hand is worth at least 10 points, and you're assured of at least eight trumps. Bid four spades or, if your partnership uses 'transfer' responses, bid four hearts, asking partner to convert to four spades. It may be beneficial if he's declarer, and the opening lead comes around to, not through, his honors.

16. December 20 — Promise Her Anything

East dealer
Both vulnerable

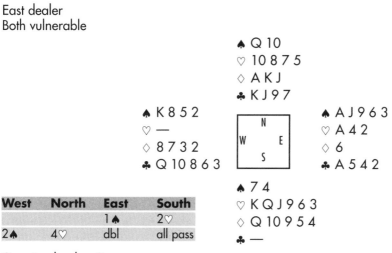

```
              ♠ Q 10
              ♡ 10 8 7 5
              ◇ A K J
              ♣ K J 9 7
 ♠ K 8 5 2              ♠ A J 9 6 3
 ♡ —           N       ♡ A 4 2
 ◇ 8 7 3 2   W   E     ◇ 6
 ♣ Q 10 8 6 3   S      ♣ A 5 4 2
              ♠ 7 4
              ♡ K Q J 9 6 3
              ◇ Q 10 9 5 4
              ♣ —
```

West	North	East	South
		1♠	2♡
2♠	4♡	dbl	all pass

Opening lead: ♠2

Dr. Ed Fitch, the president of my club, has been married 37 years. Like most husbands of long standing, he has trouble buying Christmas gifts for his wife.

'It's a case of "Promise her anything, but give her something she can exchange",' Ed says.

Ed's experience with exchanges was clear in this deal. Dummy played the ten on the first spade, and East won and switched to his singleton diamond. If you were declarer, how would you play?

Ed, South, perceived the plot: when East took the ace of trumps, he'd put his partner in with the king of spades to get a diamond ruff. So Ed won the diamond in dummy and led the king of clubs, and when East covered, Ed threw his last spade as a loser-on-loser play. West couldn't get in, and Ed later forced out the ace of trumps and claimed his game.

West had something to exchange also: if he'd correctly jumped to four spades instead of bidding two spades, he'd have lost 200 points at worst and might have been plus 790 points.

Bidding Quiz

YOU HOLD: ♠ A J 9 6 3 ♡ A 4 2 ◇ 6 ♣ A 5 4 2. Your partner opens one heart, you bid one spade and he rebids two hearts. The opponents pass. What do you say?

ANSWER: Partner has minimum values but six or more hearts; he'll make a slam if he holds as little as ♠ K 4 ♡ K Q 10 9 6 3 ◇ J 7 2 ♣ K 3. A leap to six hearts or a Blackwood bid of 4NT is reasonable. So is a bid of three clubs to be followed by a heart raise, but don't settle for a direct raise to four hearts.

17. December 21 — One Ace Suffices

South dealer
N-S vulnerable

$\spadesuit$ A 6 5 4 3 2
$\heartsuit$ 5
$\diamondsuit$ 10 7 6
$\clubsuit$ 10 8 2

West	North	East	South
			4$\heartsuit$
pass	4NT	pass	6$\heartsuit$ (!)
pass	pass	dbl	all pass

You're West. What is your opening lead?

18. December 22 — Hardly Working

North dealer
Both vulnerable

$\spadesuit$ K 10 9
$\heartsuit$ 9
$\diamondsuit$ K 6 2
$\clubsuit$ A J 7 5 4 2

$\spadesuit$ A Q J 8 2
$\heartsuit$ A 7 3
$\diamondsuit$ A 9 5 4
$\clubsuit$ 10

West	North	East	South
	1$\clubsuit$	pass	1$\spadesuit$
pass	2$\clubsuit$	pass	2$\diamondsuit$
pass	3$\spadesuit$	pass	4$\spadesuit$
all pass			

West leads the queen of hearts. Plan the play at matchpoints.

19. December 23   Extra Gift

South dealer
Both vulnerable

```
              ♠ 9 3
              ♡ 9 8 6 2
              ◇ A K 9 5
              ♣ K Q 9

              ♠ K Q J 10 7 6 5
              ♡ K Q 7
              ◇ 6
              ♣ J 8
```

West	North	East	South
			1♠
pass	2◇	pass	2♠
pass	3NT	pass	4♠
all pass			

West leads the ace of hearts and then another heart. Plan the play.

20. December 24   Hard to Find

South dealer
Both vulnerable

```
              ♠ K 10 9 6 5 2
              ♡ K 8 7 3
              ◇ 7
              ♣ 8 2

              ♠ A Q J 8 3
              ♡ A J 5
              ◇ 6 4
              ♣ K J 6
```

West	North	East	South
			1♠
2◇	4♠	all pass	

West leads the king of diamonds and shifts to a trump. Plan the play.

One Ace Suffices

South dealer
N-S vulnerable

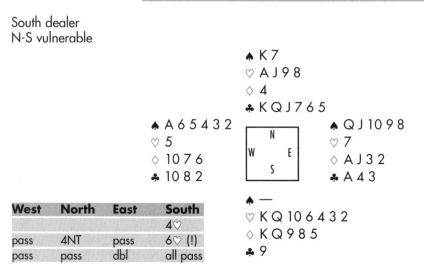

```
              ♠ K 7
              ♡ A J 9 8
              ◇ 4
              ♣ K Q J 7 6 5
♠ A 6 5 4 3 2           ♠ Q J 10 9 8
♡ 5            N        ♡ 7
◇ 10 7 6    W     E     ◇ A J 3 2
♣ 10 8 2       S        ♣ A 4 3
              ♠ —
              ♡ K Q 10 6 4 3 2
              ◇ K Q 9 8 5
              ♣ 9
```

West	North	East	South
			4♡
pass	4NT	pass	6♡ (!)
pass	pass	dbl	all pass

Opening lead: ♠A

Millard Pringle, a shy little man whose misadventures are legend, seemed troubled as I sat down at his table in a duplicate event.

'You know,' he said, 'this is the time of year when I need plenty of money. Why can't banks get into the holiday spirit and keep enough on hand? It bothers me when my checks come back marked "insufficient funds".'

'Just bid, Millard,' North sighed. So Millard opened four hearts and leaped defiantly to slam when North tried 4NT, Blackwood. After two passes, I doubled.

The contract was sound — except for an insufficiency of aces, two of which we could have cashed; but when West erred by leading the ace of spades, Millard ruffed, drew trumps, threw his club on the king of spades and led the king of clubs. When I covered, he ruffed, returned to dummy and ran the clubs to discard all five of his diamonds. Making seven!

I told Millard he should forget duplicate and play in our ten-cent-a-point "big game". He could open his own bank.

Bidding Quiz

YOU HOLD: ♠ Q J 10 9 8 ♡ 7 ◇ A J 3 2 ♣ A 4 3. You open one spade, your partner responds two hearts, you rebid two spades and he tries 2NT. The opponents pass. What do you say?

ANSWER: Though you have good intermediates in spades and two aces on the side, you have nowhere to go. Your partner's sequence promises about 11 points; with more strength, he'd have jumped to 3NT or bid a new suit to force another bid from you. Pass; game is against the odds.

18. December 22   Hardly Working

North dealer
Both vulnerable

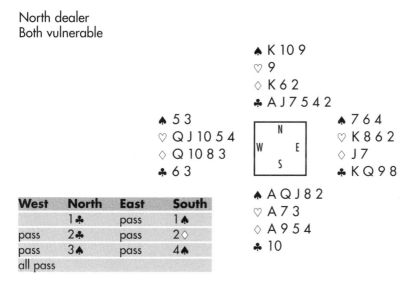

```
                     ♠ K 10 9
                     ♡ 9
                     ◇ K 6 2
                     ♣ A J 7 5 4 2
   ♠ 5 3                          ♠ 7 6 4
   ♡ Q J 10 5 4        N          ♡ K 8 6 2
   ◇ Q 10 8 3     W         E     ◇ J 7
   ♣ 6 3              S          ♣ K Q 9 8
                     ♠ A Q J 8 2
                     ♡ A 7 3
                     ◇ A 9 5 4
                     ♣ 10
```

West	North	East	South
	1♣	pass	1♠
pass	2♣	pass	2◇
pass	3♠	pass	4♠
all pass			

Opening lead: ♡Q

Not even Yuletide can put a dent in Cy the Cynic's fundamental distrust of everything and everybody. I asked Cy what the jolly old elf was bringing him for Christmas.

'You'd be jolly too,' was Cy's retort, 'if you worked only one day a year.'

At least Cy respects the value of hard work. In a duplicate event, every North-South got to four spades. Most Souths took the ace of hearts and aspired to a crossruff. They ruffed a heart, cashed the ace of clubs, ruffed a club, ruffed a heart, took the A-K of diamonds and lost a diamond. West then led a trump, killing dummy's last trump, and South lost another diamond. Making five.

Cy worked harder as declarer: he took the ace of clubs at Trick 2, ruffed a club high, led a trump to dummy, ruffed a club high, led another trump to dummy and ruffed a third club.

Cy then led a diamond to the king, drew trumps with the king, and cashed the good clubs and the ace of diamonds. He lost one diamond, making six for a top score.

Bidding Quiz

YOU HOLD: ♠ A Q J 8 2 ♡ A 7 3 ◇ A 9 5 4 ♣ 10. You open one spade, and your partner bids two spades. The opponents pass. What do you say?

ANSWER: Game is possible, and a reraise to three spades would invite. A better way to try for game, though, is to bid three diamonds. If partner has a minimum raise with fitting diamond honors — ♠ K 10 5 3 ♡ 6 5 ◇ K J 2 ♣ 8 7 6 2 — he'll jump to four spades, but he won't know to bid game if you don't show your second suit.

South dealer
Both vulnerable

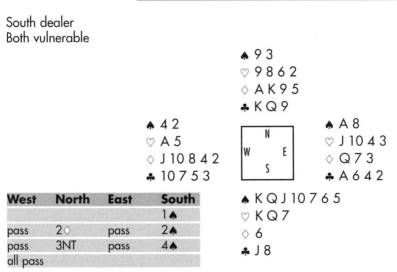

```
              ♠ 9 3
              ♡ 9 8 6 2
              ◇ A K 9 5
              ♣ K Q 9
  ♠ 4 2                      ♠ A 8
  ♡ A 5          N           ♡ J 10 4 3
  ◇ J 10 8 4 2  W     E      ◇ Q 7 3
  ♣ 10 7 5 3       S          ♣ A 6 4 2
              ♠ K Q J 10 7 6 5
              ♡ K Q 7
              ◇ 6
              ♣ J 8
```

West	North	East	South
			1♠
pass	2◇	pass	2♠
pass	3NT	pass	4♠
all pass			

Opening lead: ♡A

Unlucky Louie had forgotten to send his Christmas cards. He hastily dug a box out of his closet and, armed with his list, mailed out two dozen. It was only then he happened to inspect the inside of the card — and was chagrined to read this:

'This little card is just to say a gift from me is on its way.'

After Louie finished shopping, he still had the wherewithal to give East-West a beautiful gift. Since West had a weak hand, he led the ace of hearts against's Louie's game. East played low, but West continued with a second heart.

Louie won with the king and carelessly led a trump. When East took the ace, he led a third heart, and West ruffed and led a club to East's ace. Down one.

Louie's trump lead was too generous: since the danger of a heart ruff is clear, Louie must take the A-K of diamonds, throwing his queen of hearts. He can then lead a trump. When East wins and returns a heart, Louie ruffs high, draws trumps and loses only a club to the ace.

Bidding Quiz

YOU HOLD: ♠ A 8 ♡ J 10 4 3 ◇ Q 7 3 ♣ A 6 4 2. Your partner opens one spade, you respond two clubs, he rebids two spades and you try 2NT. Partner next bids three diamonds. What do you say?

ANSWER: Partner promises six spades, four diamonds and minimum values. You'd usually pass or return to three spades, but with two aces and a useful queen, you can be more aggressive. Bid four spades. If partner has ♠ K Q 10 6 5 4 ♡ 2 ◇ A K 8 6 ♣ 7 5, he may take eleven tricks.

20. December 24   Hard to Find

South dealer
Both vulnerable

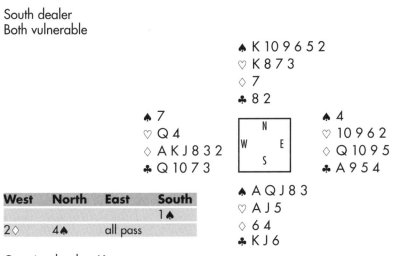

```
                        ♠ K 10 9 6 5 2
                        ♡ K 8 7 3
                        ◇ 7
                        ♣ 8 2
      ♠ 7                                    ♠ 4
      ♡ Q 4              N                   ♡ 10 9 6 2
      ◇ A K J 8 3 2   W     E                ◇ Q 10 9 5
      ♣ Q 10 7 3         S                   ♣ A 9 5 4
                        ♠ A Q J 8 3
                        ♡ A J 5
                        ◇ 6 4
                        ♣ K J 6
```

West	North	East	South
			1♠
2◇	4♠	all pass	

Opening lead: ◇K

Unlucky Louie and I were out doing some last-minute Christmas shopping for our wives — Louie says his wife has a Santa clause written into their marriage contract — when he spied a store with a sign offering "gifts for that hard-to-find person."

'Look at that,' Louie told me. 'I think I'll go in and buy something, gift-wrap it, tag it "To a good partner" and put it under the tree at the club.'

Louie has trouble finding good partners because his bad luck seems to infect most of those he plays with. As North, Louie properly leaped to four spades. East might have sacrificed at five diamonds against anybody else — East-West might lose only 500 points — but players rarely sacrifice against Louie's contracts.

West cashed a diamond and shifted to a trump, and South won in dummy and led a club to his jack. West took the queen and returned a club to East's ace, and South later lost a heart finesse with the jack. Down one.

'A misguess and a losing finesse,' Louie moaned. 'My luck hasn't changed.'

If you were South, how would you play the hand?

South should win West's trump shift in his hand, ruff his last diamond in dummy, cash the king of hearts and finesse with the jack. The finesse loses, but since West has no more hearts, he must next lead a club, saving declarer a guess, or a diamond, letting declarer discard a club from dummy and ruff in his hand.

This play gives South the extra chance of finding West with only two hearts. If West had a third heart with which to exit, South would try to guess the clubs.

21. December 27 — Headed for Trouble

South dealer
Both vulnerable

```
              ♠ 6 3
              ♡ K Q 8 6 5 4
              ◇ 5
              ♣ Q 7 6 2

              ♠ 8
              ♡ 7 3
              ◇ A Q 9 8 2
              ♣ A K J 4 3
```

West	North	East	South
			1◇
pass	1♡	1♠	2♣
3♠	4♣	pass	5♣
all pass			

West leads the five of spades, and East takes the king and leads the ace. Plan the play.

22. December 28 — Grave Concerns

South dealer
Both vulnerable

```
              ♠ 9 6 5 2
              ♡ J 3
              ◇ 8 5 2
              ♣ A Q 3 2

              ♠ A K Q 7 3
              ♡ K 7
              ◇ K 7
              ♣ K J 6 5
```

West	North	East	South
			1♠
pass	2♠	pass	4♠
all pass			

West leads the ten of clubs. Plan the play.

23. December 29   Master Planner

South dealer
N-S vulnerable

<pre>
              ♠ J 10 5
              ♡ Q J 10
              ◇ 8 7 5 3 2
              ♣ A K

              ♠ A K Q
              ♡ A K 7
              ◇ K Q 6
              ♣ Q 10 8 3
</pre>

West	North	East	South
			2♣
pass	2◇	pass	2NT
pass	6NT	all pass	

West leads the deuce of hearts. Plan the play.

24. December 31   Louie Folds Up

South dealer
Neither vulnerable

<pre>
              ♠ J 10 4 2
              ♡ J 10 9
              ◇ A Q J
              ♣ 6 5 3

              ♠ A K
              ♡ A K Q 8 7 6
              ◇ 5 2
              ♣ K 4 2
</pre>

West	North	East	South
			1♡
pass	2♡	pass	4♡
all pass			

West leads the ten of diamonds. Plan the play.

South dealer
Both vulnerable

```
                        ♠ 6 3
                        ♡ K Q 8 6 5 4
                        ◇ 5
                        ♣ Q 7 6 2
        ♠ Q 10 7 5 2                    ♠ A K J 9 4
        ♡ 9 2           ┌─────────┐     ♡ A J 10
        ◇ K J 10 7 4    │    N    │     ◇ 6 3
        ♣ 5             │ W     E │     ♣ 10 9 8
                        │    S    │
                        └─────────┘
                        ♠ 8
                        ♡ 7 3
                        ◇ A Q 9 8 2
                        ♣ A K J 4 3
```

West	North	East	South
			1◇
pass	1♡	1♠	2♣
3♠	4♣	pass	5♣
all pass			

Opening lead: ♠5

I was driving over to the club when I pulled up behind a man — an obvious fatalist — whose car bore this bumper sticker: 'Where are we going, and why am I in this handbasket?'

In this deal, South ruffed the second spade and drew trumps. When he led a heart next, West signaled with the nine to show a doubleton, and East let dummy's king win. South then came back to the ace of diamonds and tried another heart to the queen.

This time East took the ace and led a spade, giving South an unhelpful ruff-sluff, and South wound up with five trumps in his hand, one heart, a diamond and one ruff in dummy. Down three.

South was headed somewhere in a handbasket when he drew all the trumps; he can take the A-K of trumps but must lead a heart to the king next. When East ducks, South comes to the ace of diamonds to lead a second heart to the queen and ace.

South can ruff the spade return in dummy, ruff a heart and return with the queen of trumps, drawing trumps, to run the hearts and make the contract.

Bidding Quiz

YOU HOLD: ♠ Q 10 7 5 2 ♡ 9 2 ◇ K J 10 7 4 ♣ 5. With both vulnerable, the dealer, on your right, opens one diamond. You pass, the next player bids one heart, your partner overcalls one spade and opening bidder bids two clubs. What do you say?

ANSWER: Jump to four spades and try to shut out North (see the auction above). You'd like to buy the deal in four spades; your partner won't be hurt badly, if at all, in that contract.

South dealer
Both vulnerable

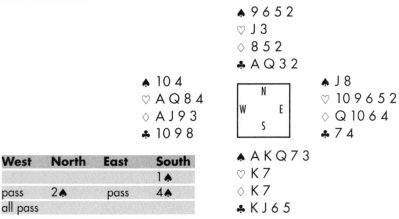

```
                        ♠ 9 6 5 2
                        ♡ J 3
                        ◇ 8 5 2
                        ♣ A Q 3 2
        ♠ 10 4                          ♠ J 8
        ♡ A Q 8 4          N            ♡ 10 9 6 5 2
        ◇ A J 9 3      W       E        ◇ Q 10 6 4
        ♣ 10 9 8           S            ♣ 7 4
                        ♠ A K Q 7 3
                        ♡ K 7
                        ◇ K 7
                        ♣ K J 6 5
```

West	North	East	South
			1♠
pass	2♠	pass	4♠
all pass			

Opening lead: ♣10

'I know they'll strike oil when they dig my grave,' Unlucky Louie told me, 'But I've given up on any good luck before then.'

Louie took the king of clubs, drew trumps, led a club to the queen and returned a diamond to his king. West won and led his last club. Louie won with the ace and tried a heart to his king, but West took two hearts and led a diamond to East's queen to beat the game.

'You'd think one red ace would be onside,' Louie sighed, 'but not in this life.'

Was Louie unlucky for once or did he misplay as usual?

Louie can strike oil in this life if he draws trumps, takes the jack and queen of clubs, and leads a heart to the king next. This play offers an extra chance: West may have the ace of hearts, but if he has the queen as well, he'll be endplayed.

As the cards lie, West wins and cashes the queen of hearts; but then West must lead a diamond, letting Louie's king score, or a heart, letting Louie ruff in dummy and pitch a diamond.

Bidding Quiz

YOU HOLD: ♠ J 8 ♡ 10 9 6 5 2 ◇ Q 10 6 4 ♣ 7 4. Your partner opens 1NT, and the next player passes. What do you say?

ANSWER: Bid two hearts, showing long hearts in a weak hand and asking partner to pass. (If you use transfer responses, bid two diamonds.) Though your suit is flimsy, your 2-5-4-2 pattern suggests playing in hearts. But if your partner is the type who won't respect a signoff and may leap to 3NT or commit some other indiscretion, pass to avoid disaster.

Master Planner

South dealer
N-S vulnerable

```
                        ♠ J 10 5
                        ♡ Q J 10
                        ◇ 8 7 5 3 2
                        ♣ A K
        ♠ 8 4 2                      ♠ 9 7 6 3
        ♡ 9 6 3 2          N         ♡ 8 5 4
        ◇ 9 4         W        E      ◇ A J 10
        ♣ J 7 5 4          S         ♣ 9 6 2
                        ♠ A K Q
                        ♡ A K 7
                        ◇ K Q 6
                        ♣ Q 10 8 3
```

West	North	East	South
			2♣
pass	2◇	pass	2NT
pass	6NT	all pass	

Opening lead: ♡2

'I get a feeling Millard's window shade doesn't go all the way to the top,' a player told me. He was talking about Millard Pringle, a little man so mannerly and reserved that he seems quite out of place at our bridge club.

'Millard hadn't been here for a week,' my friend said. 'When he showed up yesterday, he told me the left-turn indicator on his car is broken and it took him a few days to figure out a way to drive to the club by making only right turns.'

Millard must indeed be good at planning, since he made this slam in a duplicate event when many Souths failed.

Many Souths won the first heart in dummy to lead a diamond toward the K-Q-6. East played low, and South won, returned a club to dummy and led another diamond. East then took the ace and led a club, killing dummy's last entry. South had three spades, three hearts, two diamonds and three clubs, but West won the thirteenth trick with the jack of clubs.

'Millard pondered long and hard before playing to the first heart,' I was told. 'He won with the ace, led a club to the king, returned a diamond to his king, got back to dummy with the ace of clubs and led another diamond.

'East won and led a heart, but Millard took the king, cashed the queen of diamonds and got to dummy with the queen of hearts to run the diamonds.'

'Nicely played,' I smiled.

'Sure was,' my friend agreed, 'especially for a guy who once told me he moved because he heard most accidents happen close to home.'

24. December 31 | Louie Folds Up

South dealer
Neither vulnerable

```
              ♠ J 10 4 2
              ♡ J 10 9
              ◇ A Q J
              ♣ 6 5 3
  ♠ Q 9 6                      ♠ 8 7 5 3
  ♡ 5 3 2         N            ♡ 4
  ◇ 10 9 8 3   W     E         ◇ K 7 6 4
  ♣ A 8 7         S            ♣ Q J 10 9
              ♠ A K
              ♡ A K Q 8 7 6
              ◇ 5 2
              ♣ K 4 2
```

West	North	East	South
			1♡
pass	2♡	pass	4♡
all pass			

Opening lead: ◇ 10

In the lounge after an evening team game, Unlucky Louie, who had fared poorly, was trying out a new concoction Marvin our bartender called a Card Table.

'Two of 'em,' said Marvin, 'and your legs fold up under you.'

Midway through his first (and only) Card Table, Louie brought up this deal.

'I finessed with the queen of diamonds,' he said, 'and East won and shifted to clubs. West had the ace, and the contract folded up under me.'

While Louie finishes his drink, decide how you'd play the hand.

South has the material for ten winners but must not let East get in for a fatal club shift. South takes the ace of diamonds and the top spades, leads a trump to dummy and returns the jack of spades. When East plays low, South throws his last diamond.

West takes the queen and leads a trump, and South wins in dummy and leads the queen of diamonds, planning to throw a club if East plays low. No matter who has the king of diamonds, South's contract is safe.

Bidding Quiz

YOU HOLD: ♠ J 10 4 2 ♡ J 10 9 ◇ A Q J ♣ 6 5 3. Your partner opens one heart, you raise to two hearts and he next bids three clubs. The opponents pass. What do you say?

ANSWER: Partner's three clubs is a try for game, and since you have 9 points — a maximum for your raise — you can accept. To jump to four hearts with poor holdings in clubs and hearts would be wrong, though. Bid three diamonds, suggesting diamond strength, or bid 3NT.

More Bridge Titles from Master Point Press

ABTA Book of the Year Award Winners

25 Bridge Conventions You Should Know
by Barbara Seagram and Marc Smith
(foreword by Eddie Kantar)
192pp., PB   Can $21.95   US $16.95

Eddie Kantar teaches Modern Bridge Defense
Eddie Kantar teaches Advanced Bridge Defense
by Eddie Kantar
each 240pp., PB   Can $27.95   US $19.95

Also available in Interactive CD-ROM Editions
Modern Bridge Defense   Can $69.95   US $49.95
Advanced Bridge Defense   Can $69.95   US $49.95

The Bridge Technique Series
by David Bird & Marc Smith
each 64pp. PB   Can $7.95   US $5.95

Deceptive Card Play	Planning in Suit Contracts
Defensive Signaling	Reading the Cards
Eliminations and Throw-Ins	Safety Plays
Entry Management	Squeezes for Everyone
Planning in Defense	Tricks with Finesses
Planning in Notrump Contracts	Tricks with Trumps

25 Bridge Myths Exposed by David Bird
200 pp., PB   Can $19.95   US $15.95

Around the World in 80 Hands by Zia Mahmood with David Burn
256 pp., PB   Can $22.95   US $16.95

A Study in Silver A second collection of bridge stories by David Silver
128 pp., PB   Can $12.95   US$ 9.95

Becoming a Bridge Expert by Frank Stewart
300 pp., PB   Can $27.95   US $19.95

Best of Bridge Today Digest by Matthew and Pamela Granovetter
192 pp., PB   Can $19.95   US $14.95

Bridge Conventions in Depth by Matthew and Pamela Granovetter
240 pp., PB   Can $27.95   US $19.95

Bridge Problems for a New Millennium by Julian Pottage
160 pp., PB   Can $14.95   US $11.95

Bridge the Silver Way by David Silver and Tim Bourke
192 pp., PB   Can $19.95   US $14.95

Bridge Squeezes for Everyone* *Yes, even you! by David Bird
220 pp., PB   Can $24.95   US $17.95

Bridge: 25 Steps to Learning 2/1 by Paul Thurston (foreword by Eric Kokish)
192 pp., PB   Can $19.95   US $15.95

25 Ways to Take More Tricks as Declarer by Barbara Seagram and David Bird
200 pp., PB   Can $19.95   US $15.95

Bridge: 25 Ways to Compete in the Bidding .by Barbara Seagram and Marc Smith
220 pp., PB   Can $21.95   US $16.95

Bridge, Zia... and me by Michael Rosenberg (foreword by Zia Mahmood)
192 pp., PB   Can $19.95   US $15.95

Challenge Your Declarer Play by Danny Roth
128 pp., PB   Can $12.95   US $ 9.95

Classic Kantar a collection of bridge humor by Eddie Kantar
192 pp., PB   Can $19.95   US $14.95

Competitive Bidding in the 21st Century by Marshall Miles
254 pp., PB   Can $22.95   US. $16.95

Countdown to Winning Bridge by Tim Bourke and Marc Smith
192 pp., PB   Can $19.95   US $14.95

Easier Done Than Said Brilliancy at the Bridge Table by Prakash K. Paranjape
128 pp., PB   Can $15.95   US $12.95

Eddie Kantar Teaches Topics in Declarer Play by Eddie Kantar
240 pp., PB   Can $27.95   US $19.95
Also available
on CD-ROM   Can $69.95   US $49.95

For Love or Money The Life of a Bridge Journalist by Mark Horton and Brian Senior
189 pp., PB   Can $22.95   US $16.95

Following the LAW by Larry Cohen
192 pp., PB   Can $19.95   US $15.95

Focus On Declarer Play by Danny Roth
128 pp., PB   Can $12.95   US $9.95

Focus On Defence by Danny Roth
128 pp., PB   Can $12.95   US $9.95

Focus On Bidding by Danny Roth
160 pp., PB   Can $14.95   US $11.95

Frank Stewart's Bridge Club by Frank Stewart
200 pp., PB   Can $21.95   US $16.95

How to Play Bridge with Your Spouse... and Survive! by Roselyn Teukolsky
192 pp., PB   Can $19.95   US $14.95

I Shot my Bridge Partner by Matthew Granovetter
384 pp., PB   Can $19.95   US $14.95

Inferences at Bridge by Marshall Miles
192 pp., PB   Can $22.95   US $16.95

Larry Cohen's Bidding Challenge by Larry Cohen
192 pp., PB   Can $19.95   US $15.95

Murder at the Bridge Table by Matthew Granovetter
320 pp., PB   Can $19.95   US $14.95

Playing with the Bridge Legends by Barnet Shenkin (forewords by Zia and Michael Rosenberg)
240 pp., PB   Can $24.95   US $17.95

The Pocket Guide to Bridge by Barbara Seagram and Ray Lee
64 pp., PB   Can $9.95   US $7.95

Richelieu Plays Bridge by Robert F. MacKinnon
220 pp., PB   Can $24.95   US $17.95

Saints and Sinners The St. Titus Bridge Challenge by David Bird & Tim Bourke
192 pp., PB   Can $19.95   US $14.95

Samurai Bridge A tale of old Japan by Robert F. MacKinnon
256 pp., PB   Can $ 22.95   US $16.95

Tales out of School 'Bridge 101' and other stories by David Silver
128 pp., PB   Can $ 12.95   US $9.95

The Bridge Bum: My Life and Play by Alan Sontag
240 pp., PB   Can $26.95   US $19.95

The Bridge Magicians by Mark Horton and Radoslaw Kielbasinski
248 pp., PB   Can $24.95   US $18.95

The Bridge Player's Bedside Book edited by Tony Forrester
256 pp., HC   Can $27.95   US $19.95

The Bridge World's 'Test Your Play' by Jeff Rubens
164 pp., PB   Can.$14.95   US $11.95

There Must Be A Way... 52 challenging bridge hands by Andrew Diosy (foreword by Eddie Kantar)
96 pp., PB   Can $9.95   US $9.95

Thinking on Defense The art of visualization at bridge by Jim Priebe
197 pp., PB   Can $ 19.95   US $15.95

To Bid or Not to Bid by Larry Cohen
248 pp., PB   Can $24.95   US $17.95

Win the Bermuda Bowl with Me by Jeff Meckstsroth and Marc Smith
188 pp., PB   Can $24.95   US $17.95

World Class — conversations with the bridge masters by Marc Smith
288 pp., PB   Can $24.95   US $17.95